BEST EVER Crafts

Vivienne Bolton

DP

DEMPSEY
PARR

BEST EVER Crafts

Design Team
Design Study

Photography
Patrick Spillane

Photographic Co-ordinator
Liz Spillane

Styling
Bianca Boulton

Project Management
Kate Miles

The publishers would like to thank Inscribe Ltd., Bordon, Hants. for providing the art materials used in these projects & Sophie Boulton for her assistance

First published in 1998 by
Dempsey Parr
13 Whiteladies Road, Clifton, Bristol
BS8 1PB

24681097531

Produced by Miles Kelly Publishing Ltd
Unit 11, Bardfield Centre, Great Bardfield, Essex CM7 4SL

British Library Cataloguing-in-Publication Data
A catalogue record for this book is available from the British Library

ISBN 1-84084-216-4

Printed in China

BEST EVER Crafts

CONTENTS

DRIED SEEDPODS AND STALKS

Seedpod Jewellery

Collect seedpods and hollow stalks from the garden in the summer, and stand them up in a jar to dry in a warm airy spot. You will need a large darning needle to make a hole through the seedpods once they have dried. The beads in the necklaces are made from cut lengths of dried stalks. Thread them using the darning needle and decorate them with paint. Gold and brown paint have been used on these beads to accentuate the natural look. Beads painted in bright colours and decorated with glitter would make an attractive necklace.

You will need:

Selection of seedpods and stalks

Scissors

Paint

Paint-brush

Darning needle

Thread

Felt tip pens

Elastic band

Check with an adult before you pick plants and stems to dry.

1 To make this necklace you will need a
   few dried hollow plant stems, some small
   fir-cones and seedpods. Begin by cutting
   the plant stems into bead-size lengths.
   Paint the bead lengths, fir cones and
   seedpods gold. When your beads are dry use
   the darning needle to make suitable holes
   through them and thread together using one
   seedpod to every three plant stems to make a
   necklace or bracelet.

2 This delicate looking necklace is made
   simply from some dried hollow plant
   stems. Once you have cut the stems into
   bead-sized lengths, decorate the beads using
   brown felt tip pens or brown paint. Thread
   them together using the darning needle.

3 A small bunch of twigs is used to make this
   pendant. Choose straight twigs that don't
   have any thorns or snags. Use an elastic
   band to hold them together in a neat
   bunch to form a pendant. Paint the pendant
   gold; it may be necessary to give it two coats.
   Once the paint had dried attach a length of
   thread to the pendant and it is ready to wear.

Plate Gardens

Wile away a rainy afternoon making a miniature garden. These realistic-looking gardens are laid out on dinner plates. You could create an imaginary garden or recreate a section of your own garden. Have a look around outside for plants and tiny flowers to use to decorate your plate garden. Make fences from lollysticks or twigs and use your imagination to help you create miniature copies of real life objects. Use tiny pebbles to make a garden path. See if you can find some miniature ornaments that will be the right scale for garden statues.

You will need:

Plate

Sand

Potting compost

Pebbles

Sticks and thread

Dried flowers and moss

Selection of leaves and flowers

Modelling clay

Salt

Scissors

Paper

1 Place a layer of sand on a plate and cover it with a layer of potting compost. Use small pebbles to lay a path. Make some beanpoles from twigs tied with thread and press them firmly into the earth. Use some moss to create a hedge.

2 The garden is now ready for the vegetables to be 'planted'. A small leaved plant stem has been wound round the beanpoles, and a slightly larger leaved plant stem is laid on the earth. The carrot leaves are made from maidenhair fern with clay models of vegetables and garden tools laid amongst the leaves.

3 The washing is drying in a corner of this sweet little flower garden. Begin with a layer of sand on a plate and cover that with a thin layer of potting compost. Use some checked paper to make the path and two long twigs tied with a piece of string to make the washing line. A piece of paper is cut to make the white picket fence. Now cut some paper clothes to hang on the line.

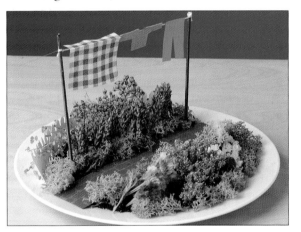

4 The washing is hung on the line and the garden in now full of flowers and plants. Use moss as plants and some dried flowers pressed into the earth.

5 This winter scene is very effective. Place a layer of sand on the plate and make a snowman from modelling clay. Plant a few moss bushes and press some twigs into the sand. When your model is arranged pour salt over everything to create a snowscene.

Bird Feeders

Whether you live in the town or the country there will be wild birds about. You can easily attract the birds to your garden or windowsill by placing some wild bird seed in a small bird feeder where cats cannot get to it. The birds will enjoy a good feed and you will learn to recognize the different species. The bird feeder is made from an empty milk carton. If you hang it near a window you can keep an eye on the birds while you are out of sight, indoors. You might also want to thread some peanuts on a string and hang them out for the birds.

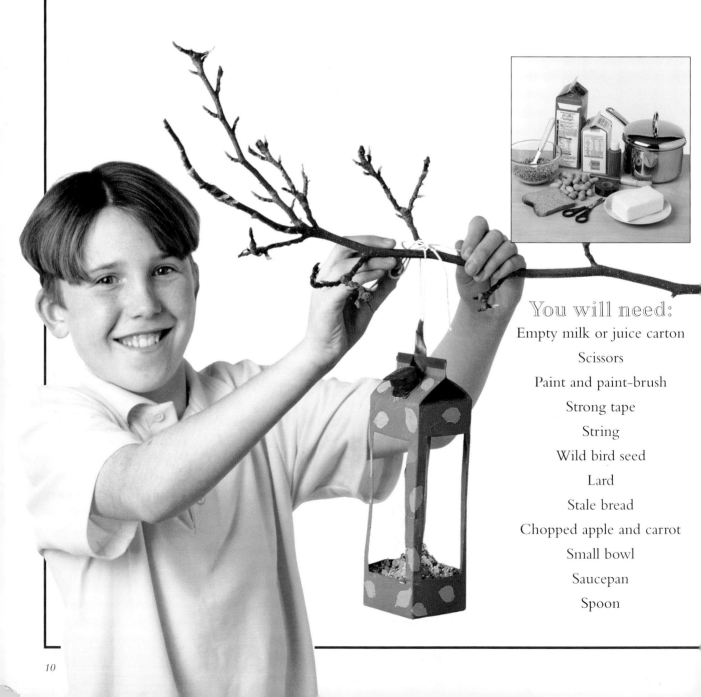

You will need:

Empty milk or juice carton

Scissors

Paint and paint-brush

Strong tape

String

Wild bird seed

Lard

Stale bread

Chopped apple and carrot

Small bowl

Saucepan

Spoon

1 Making this bird feeder is a good way to recycle a milk or juice carton. Cut away most of the sides of the carton leaving space at the base to hold the bird seed.

2 Once you have got the shape of the bird feeder right you can paint it. Choose a colour that will blend in with the surroundings and not frighten off the birds.

3 When the paint is dry you can decorate the bird feeder. Attach a piece of strong tape in a loop to the top of the feeder and fill the base with some wild bird seed.

4 Hang your bird feeder in a place, safe from the reach of cats. Thread some peanuts on a piece of string and hang that up alongside the feeder.

5 To make a bird seed ball you will need a saucepan and some lard, available from a supermarket. Melt the lard in a saucepan over a low heat (you may need an adult to help you with this). Collect the rest of your ingredients together. You can use old bread and wild bird seed and could always add some chopped carrot, assorted nuts or apple to the mixture.

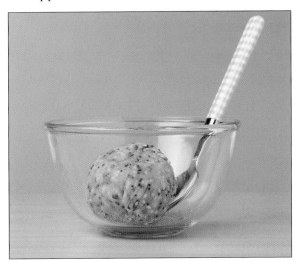

6 Break a slice of bread into small pieces and place them in a bowl; pour over the melted lard. Add the wild bird seed and mix well together. As the mixture cools you will be able to form it into a ball. Push a piece of string into the centre of the mixture. Once it has hardened you will be able to hang the ball up with the string, alongside your bird feeder.

FLOWERS AND LEAVES

Pressed Flowers

Flower pressing was a popular activity among ladies in the nineteenth century. Nowadays flower pressing is regaining popularity as a hobby. If you have a garden it is easy to find flowers to press, although you should check with an adult before you pick any flowers. Pressing flowers dries them out, flattening them and leaving a little of the original colour. This creates a material you can use to decorate writing paper and greeting cards, and if you press enough flowers you could create a whole picture or cover a small box. Once you have pressed your flowers, store them flat between layers of tissue paper in a box in a dry, airy place to save their colour.

When picking flowers to press make sure that they have no insects in them, and that the petals are perfect, not torn or brown.

Put the flowers in your flowerpress or in tissue between the pages of a thick book, as soon after picking as possible.

1 Pressing flowers is a wonderful hobby. Press the flowers flat in a flowerpress or use an old book. The flowers will need to be left in place for quite a few weeks before they are ready to use.

2 Pressed flowers can be used to decorate greeting cards. You can buy prepared cards to decorate or make your own from nice paper. Spend a little time trying out designs by laying different pressed flowers and leaves on the paper. When you are happy with your design use a little glue to attach the pressed flowers to the card. You may want to paint on a little varnish to give the picture a high gloss finish.

3 For a rose picture, press a whole rose carefully in your flowerpress. Leave it for a few weeks until most of the moisture has dried out. Choose a small frame and place the pressed rose in it. If you press lots of flowers you may have enough to cover a small box.

Making Paper

Paper is made from recycled fibrous material, this could be newspaper, computer paper, sugar paper, mashed up pot pourri or leaves. You will need a small picture frame and an adult with a staple gun to help you make a paper making tray. The size of the picture frame will be the size of the sheet of paper you make, so bear that in mind when you choose your frame. Once you have mastered the art of paper making you can experiment with colours and textures. Try laying pressed flowers on the wet sheet of formed paper or using different coloured material. Food colouring can be used to colour paper to good effect.

You will need:

Staple gun

Fabric

Wooden picture frame

Torn up pieces of
sugar paper

Kitchen blender

Container

Newspaper

Kitchen cloths

Rolling pin

1 To make a paper making frame ask an adult to staple a piece of fabric taut over the back of a wooden picture frame.

2 Tear the paper up into small pieces and place it in the blender. Cover well with water. Blend until the paper is well mashed. Ask an adult for help with the electric blender.

3 Pour the well watered down paper pulp into a container large enough to take the paper-making frame. You will need enough pulp to half fill the container.

4 Lower the frame into the pulpy water and swish it around getting a layer of paper pulp into the frame. You may need to do this a few times to get the pulp evenly spread across the frame.

5 Lift the frame out of the water. Cover the work surface with old newspaper and lay a kitchen cloth on top of it.

6 In one movement tip the pulp out of the frame. You may need to give the frame a knock to get the pulp out. Place another kitchen cloth on top of the paper and press it down firmly.

7 Press evenly and firmly down on the kitchen cloth using a rolling pin. This will remove the excess water. You have now made a sheet of paper.

8 In this picture there are two sheets of hand made paper. You will need to practise to get the amounts of pulp right and learn how to spread the pulp evenly across the frame.

OAK-GALLS, FRUITS AND PETALS
Making Ink

People have been making ink since they could draw and write. Some of the oldest books in existence were written with ink made with oak-galls - try making some for yourself. Oak-galls are the swellings caused by gall wasp larvae burrowing into leaf buds. They are found on oak trees in autumn. Give them a good shake to ensure the insects have hatched and left home. You can also use coloured fruit juice as ink – blackcurrants, raspberries and mulberries all stain in shades of red, while daffodil petals make a yellow ink. If you wanted to be secretive, try writing a letter in lemon juice. Once the writing has dried, you can bring up the message by ironing the paper with a warm iron. The message will colour brown and you will be able to read it.

You will need:
Oak-galls, soft fruit or petals

Pestle and mortar

Jar

Water

Rusty nail

Piece of muslin

Lemon

Paper and pen

1 You will need to find some oak-galls to make this ink. Pick them in the autumn after the insects have flown. Two or three oak-galls will make a couple of tablespoons of ink. Put the oak-galls in a mortar and crush them using a pestle.

3 You can use dark coloured fruit juice as ink. Use a dipping pen to write with. Blackcurrants, raspberries and mulberries will give shades of red and you can make a yellow from daffodil petals. Try different vegetables – beetroot gives a good colour.

2 Place the crushed oak-galls in a jar and add a tablespoon of water for each one and one rusty nail. Leave the mixture to stand, uncovered. After an hour you will notice that the liquid begins to change colour. By the next day it should be quite dark and in a week it should be nearly black. Strain the ink through a piece of muslin and it is ready to use.

4 To make invisible ink you can use lemon juice. Squeeze the juice of half a lemon into a small container. Use a dipping pen or a thin paint-brush. Write your message on a sheet of paper and leave it to dry. To make the writing visible you will need to iron it, the writing will turn a brown colour with the heat from the iron. Ask an adult for help with the iron.

Crunchy Salads

Sprouted seeds make good salads. They are crunchy to eat and packed full of vitamins. You could set up a small sprout farm on the kitchen windowsill and provide the family with fresh salad ingredients all through the winter months. Alfalfa seeds are small and tasty while mung bean seeds are larger. You can sprout sunflower seeds to make large and crunchy sprouts. Ask at your local wholefood shop for a list of suitable seeds for sprouting.

You will need:
Small piece of muslin

Saucer to draw around

Pen and scissors

Jam jar

Elastic band

Seeds for sprouting

Water

1 To sprout seeds you will need a jar with a muslin lid (so that the seeds can be washed and drained without losing any down the sink). You will need a piece of muslin and a large saucer; use the saucer to mark out a circle on the muslin.

3 Place one large spoonful of suitable seed in the jam jar (we have used mung beans). Cover the seeds with water and leave them to soak for two hours.

2 Cut away the excess fabric. This will be the lid of the jam jar. You will need an elastic band to hold the fabric onto the jam jar. You are now ready to start sprouting seeds.

4 Lay the muslin over the jam jar and hold it in place with an elastic band. You will need to rinse away the water. Wash the sprouts with water three times a day and watch them grow. When the sprouts are long enough to eat and before the leaves appear, take them out of the jar. Give them a good wash in clean water and use them in salads for a crunchy fresh taste.

Purchase seeds for sprouting from your local wholefood shop. Do not sprout seeds purchased for growing in the garden, they sometimes have chemicals on them to prevent pests eating them and can be harmful to people as well.

Twig Furniture

Rustic miniature furniture can be made from twigs and sticks found in the garden. You will need a sturdy pair of scissors and good strong glue for this. A set of miniature garden furniture could be useful when decorating a plate garden, or to sit outside a doll's house. If you have a miniature teddy bear or doll use it to gauge how large the furniture should be. The early American settlers made real furniture for their cabins from roughly hewn wood. You could make a model cabin and decorate it with rustic furniture and found items from the garden.

You will need:

Sticks and twigs

Kitchen scissors

Glue

Some fabric for cushions or blankets

1 To make the chair you will need some sturdy twigs for the legs and back, and thin twigs to make the seat. It is a good idea to lay the sticks out flat and check their shape. Check that the cut pieces fit together as you go along. When you are happy with the shape of your chair use strong glue to stick it together.

2 For the table choose four good straight twigs to use as legs. Make a frame and glue one leg to each corner. Make the top by laying the pieces down on the work surface and pour a line of strong glue on each end of the tabletop. Leave it to dry. When the frame and the table top have dried you can assemble your table.

3 Make the bed head and foot of the bed first. The bed head is made by making a glued frame with diagonal pieces set in. The foot of the bed is the shape of a letter 'H'. When the glue has set, fix long twigs between the two ends. Use a piece of fabric to make a mattress and quilt to cover the bed.

Desert Gardens

Growing a desert garden can be most rewarding. Garden centres and florists stock cactus plants. It is a good idea to check what plants are available before you buy a suitable planter. You will need a sunny windowsill on which to place your planted desert garden. Choose a pot large enough to hold a few cacti so that the overall impression is of a small corner of the desert. When you have planted the cacti, decorate the scene with some stones to resemble boulders.

You will need:

Plant pot

Gravel

Old spoon or small garden trowel

Cactus potting compost

Cactus plants

Suitable gloves

Selection of stones and crytals

White sand

1 Begin by placing a layer of gravel. This will provide drainage for the plants.

2 Next add a good layer of suitable cactus potting compost. Press it down firmly.

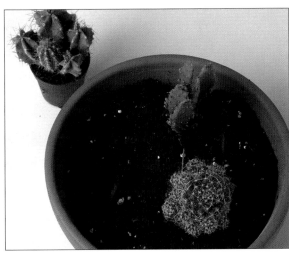

3 Dig small holes in the compost and plant the cacti. Remember to wear gloves.

4 Create a realistic-looking desert scene with some attractive stones and crystals.

5 When you are happy with the look of your desert garden, cover the compost with a layer of white sand. This will give the impression of desert sand.

Cactus plants need special growing conditions. Keep them hot in summer; place the desert garden on a windowsill that gets sunlight most of the day. Water your plants sparingly and regularly.

Always wear thick gloves when handling cacti as the spines and prickles are sharp.

Bottle Gardens

Create a miniature oasis in a bottle. All you need to start a bottle garden is a large, empty sweet jar and some potting compost. Choose plants which will stay quite small; ask for assistance at your local garden centre or florist. Some garden centres have bottle garden departments where they sell small plants suitable for this enclosed, small environment. Bottle gardens should never have the sun shining directly onto them (they would get too hot), but they do need to be in a light situation. Keep the soil moist. You may not need to water often if the lid is kept firmly on. Feed your bottle garden every two weeks during the summer. Decorate it using glass paints and outliners. Choose a gold outliner for a stylish pattern or use black outliner and coloured paint to create a stained glass effect on the exterior of the bottle.

You will need:

Sticks

Old spoon

Wire

Kitchen sponge

Cotton wool

A large empty sweet jar

Pebbles or gravel

Suitable potting compost

Suitable plants

Glass paints outliner

Glass paint

1 Begin by making some suitable bottle garden tools. For a digging tool, use an old spoon attached with wire to a long stick. Use a piece of kitchen sponge wired onto a stick to press the earth down when you are planting. Lastly, you will need a cleaning tool. For this use a piece of cotton wool wired onto a stick (you may need a few of these to tidy up the bottle garden once it is planted).

2 Place a thin layer of pebbles or gravel in the base of the bottle. This will provide drainage for the bottle garden plants.

3 Cover the pebbles with a thick layer of potting compost. Press the compost down gently using your sponge tool.

4 Use the digging tool to place individual plants in position. Press the compost down firmly around the plants, taking care not to damage their roots.

5 Use the cotton wool tool to clean up the sides of the bottle garden. Wipe away any smears or pieces of compost that have stuck to the sides of the jar.

6 Your bottle garden is now ready to decorate. Choose a simple pattern and mark it out with the outliner. The stained glass effect will resemble a mini-conservatory.

When choosing plants for your bottle garden choose low growing varieties. Keep the compost moist but do not overwater. Feed your bottle garden every two weeks in the growing season.

RECYCLED
Plant Pots

Don't throw away those empty yoghurt cartons and margarine tubs, recycle them into these stylish plant pots. Create a set of matching planters for the kitchen windowsill using bright, eyecatching colours and white dots and plant them up with useful herbs. A design of white hearts or flowers would look good in the bedroom with a leafy, green plant in it, or you could follow the step-by-step instructions and paint a green planter decorated with leaves and flowers.

1 Paint on the base coat. Be sure to cover the pot completely. When it is dry check that the paint is even. You may need two coats to cover the pot well.

2 Paint a thin border at the base of the pot, then paint the rim. When this is dry, paint on the leaves in the same colour.

3 Practise painting the flowers on a sheet of rough paper before you paint them on your pot.

4 When flowers are completely dry, paint on the white and yellow centres.

5 These yellow yoghurt cartons don't need much decorating. Paint them in bright colours to grow cress in or use them for small plants.

You will need:

A selection of recycled pots and tubs

Acrylic paint in a variety of colours

Paint-brushes

Paper towel or a cloth in case of spills

Acrylic paint will not stick to the tubs and pots unless they are spotlessly clean. Wash all your recycled pots in warm soapy water and rinse them well before drying them with a clean cloth.

Cover your work surface with newspaper before you begin painting.

VEG, MEAT AND FISH
Burgers

Follow our easy recipes for burgers which are quick to prepare and delicious to eat. Make them from minced meat, cooked beans, tofu or fish. There is a recipe to suit every taste. For a professional look serve your burgers with a garnish such as a slice of lemon, cress or sliced tomato and lettuce.

You will need:

Ingredients

Bowl

Potato masher

Wooden spoon

Frying pan

Plates and cutlery to serve

Bean Burgers:	Tofu Burgers:	Fish burgers:	Lamb burgers:
1 can of black-eyed beans	250g block of tofu, chopped	155g tin pilchards in tomato sauce	250g minced lamb
1 small chopped onion, fried	1 small chopped onion, fried	1 cup wholemeal breadcrumbs	1 teaspoon mixed herbs
1 teaspoon mixed herbs	2 teaspoons fresh or dried parsley	1 small chopped onion, fried	salt and pepper to taste
1 egg	1 cup wholemeal breadcrumbs	1 teaspoon mixed herbs	1 egg
1 cup of wholemeal breadcrumbs	2 teaspoons soya sauce	Flour to roll the finished burgers in	half a cup of wholemeal breadcrumbs
Flour to roll the finished burgers in	Sesame seeds to roll finished burgers in	A little oil for frying	Flour to roll the finished burgers in
A little oil for frying	A little oil for frying		A little oil for frying

1 Empty the beans or other main ingredient into the bowl and mash them well.

2 Add the rest of the ingredients and mix well with a wooden spoon. Use your hands to shape the mixture into burger shapes and roll in flour.

3 Fry in a little hot oil, serve on a burger bun. A tasty meal, easily prepared.

Always have an adult in the kitchen when you are cooking on top of the stove.

Wash your hands before preparing food.

AIR HARDENING CLAY
Egg Cups

Boiled eggs for breakfast will never be the same again with one of these fun egg cups. They are made from air-hardening clay. Make a Humpty Dumpty egg cup for a young brother or sister, or choose a more stylish crown or simple shape painted to match your breakfast plates. Make a set of egg cups, one for each member of the family, decorated to suit their hobbies or interests.

You will need:
A block of air hardening clay

Clay modelling tool

Tray to stand the egg cup on while it is drying

Acrylic paints

Paint-brush

Varnish

1 Begin by shaping a block of clay to be the wall for Humpty to sit on.

3 When the model is completely dry, you can decorate it. Paint one colour at a time allowing each shade to dry.

2 Make the legs and arms from sausage shapes and use an egg to gauge the size of the cup. Once you have made your model, leave it to dry for 24 hours.

4 Varnish the egg cup when the paint is completely dry.

Before you begin, cover your work surface with newspaper or a plastic cloth – working with clay can be a messy business. It is a good idea to work on a tray which will enable you to carry your finished item to a safe place to dry.

If you cannot get hold of air hardening clay, make Humpty from salt and flour dough: mix 2 cups of plain flour and 1 cup of fine salt, add 1 cup of water and mix well. Knead for 5 minutes, then the dough will be ready for use.

SALT AND FLOUR
Dough Baskets

U se salt and flour dough to make a basket for bread rolls or fruit. Once baked in the oven the basket is ready for you to paint and varnish. Flower shapes or dough fruit make very good decoration. Use animal-shaped biscuit cutters to make dough pets with the leftover dough. Always bake the pieces thoroughly and allow them to get quite cold before you paint them.

Salt and flour dough is not good to eat, keep it away from young brothers and sisters.

Always wash out your paint and varnish brushes, keep them clean and ready to use.

You will need:
Wooden spoon and large bowl

2 cups of flour

1 cup of salt

1 cup of water

A little spare flour

Rolling pin

Knife

Shallow oven-proof dish

Aluminium foil to line your dish

Acrylic paint and brushes

Water-based varnish

1 Use a wooden spoon to mix the flour, salt and water well. When it forms a ball take it out of the bowl and knead it for 5 minutes. Sprinkle some flour onto the worksurface to prevent the dough sticking as you work.

2 When the dough is smooth roll it out onto a floured surface and cut it into strips about 2 cm wide.

3 Cover a bowl with aluminium foil. Weave the strips into the bowl. Make the cherries from small balls of dough. Use a short piece of thin wire or two small sticks for the cherry stalks.

4 Bake the basket for 4 hours at 130°C, gas mark 1 to 2 or until it is completely dry.

5 When your model is cool take it out of the bowl, paint and varnish.

Toast Racks

Brighten up the breakfast table with one of these easy to make toast racks. They are made from recycled grocery boxes and torn up strips of newspaper. Before you begin have a look around the kitchen and choose a colour and style that will match.

Some toast racks have space for butter pats and jam while others only have room for toast. When you have made one of the simple shapes you could try something a little different. A nicely made toast rack would make a good gift for a friend or neighbour.

You will need:

Card from a cardboard box

Sturdy scissors

PVA glue

Water

Torn up pieces of newspaper

Acrylic paint and brushes

1 Use card from a grocery box to cut out an oval-shaped base and four racks. You will need a pair of sturdy scissors.

2 Use the blade of the scissors to score the card then tear out slots for the racks. Remember to leave enough space for the slices of toast between the racks.

3 Glue the racks into place and set aside until the glue has dried.

4 Mix an equal quantity of PVA (white) glue with water. Glue small torn pieces of newspaper all over your model.

5 When the toast rack is completely dry it is ready to decorate. Use acrylic paint and a design that matches the shape of your toast rack.

Remember to protect your work surface with newspaper or a vinyl cloth.

If you don't have any glue, get an adult to help you make some. Mix two cups of water and one cup of flour in a saucepan and cook it gently, stirring all the time, until it is thick, creamy and sticky.

Frames

F rame a special photograph in one of these pretty frames. They are made out of card from a grocery box and covered with aluminium foil. Choose a simple shape and expect a few discards while you master the method. Simple patterns are best to decorate the frames: flowers, hearts or stars for example. Have a look around the kitchen and you may find coloured foil you could recycle. The gold foil frame is made with recycled margarine tub foil! Try sprucing up an old picture frame by covering it with foil.

You will need:

Thick card (from a grocery box)

Ruler

Strong scissors

Foil

Glue

Pencil and ball point pen

Remember foil is made from metal and can be sharp – take care.

1 Use a photograph to measure how large the frame should be. Cut out the foil shape a few centimetres larger than the card frame.

2 Spread the card frame with glue and making sure there is no glue on your fingers, gently press the foil over the frame. Tuck the edges in well, smoothing the foil carefully.

3 Cover the backing of the frame with foil.

4 Attach the frame to the backing with glue on three sides, leaving an opening to slip in the photograph.

5 Use the ball point pen to mark the design onto the frame.

GLASS AND PAINT
Glass Painting

Glass painting is a great hobby and a good way of recycling empty jam jars and bottles or personalising glasses to give away as gifts or use in the home. Glass paints also work well on plastic containers, so collect a few large plastic containers and decorate them for use in the kitchen, for storing dried pasta or beans. Glass paints come in a wide variety of colours and are easy to use. Experiment with simple designs at first. Always try out your ideas on paper before painting on glass. If you make a mistake on the glass wipe the paint off quickly and start again.

1 Before you begin wash and dry the glass. Use the black outliner to mark up the pattern. Be sure there are no gaps for the glass paint to escape through. When the black outliner is completely dry use a dry brush to dip into the glass paint. Wash the brush well between colours and dry it before dipping it into the next colour.

2 Use the gold outliner on its own for this stylish look. Think about what will be in the container when deciding on colour and design.

3 Save tiny jars to decorate and fill with jam.

You will need:
Selection of glasses, jars and bottles
Outliners in black, gold and silver
Paint-brush
Water-soluble glass paints
Kitchen towel for spills

Remember to protect your work surface with newspaper before you begin.

Always make sure the glasses and jars are washed and dried with a clean cloth before you begin to decorate them.

Indoor Picnics

Rainy days are perfect for indoor picnics. Fill the hamper with egg rolls, cheese and potato pasties and delicious jam tarts. Everyone will enjoy the pasties which are easy to make and very filling. Use the leftover pastry to make a few jam tarts. Simply cut out circles with a biscuit cutter, place in a greased bun tin with a small spoonful of jam in each one. Bake for 12 minutes at 180°C, 350°F, gas mark 4. For the rolls filling, hardboil an egg and when it is cool, chop it up and mix it with a small spoonful of mayonnaise. Spread it on rolls with some cress for a picnic treat.

You will need:

Bowl

Tablespoon

Rolling pin

Saucer

Knife

Baking tray

Fork

Pastry brush

Recipe for cheese & onion pasties

Pastry:

250g plain flour

125g margarine or butter

A little water

A little extra flour

Pasty filling:

1 cup of cooked diced potato

1 medium onion, chopped

75g cheddar cheese, grated

Salt and pepper

1 egg, beaten

1 Make the pastry first, place the flour and margarine (or butter) in a bowl, use your fingers to mix it until it looks like breadcrumbs. Add a tablespoon of water and mix well, you may need another tablespoon or two of water but add it a little at a time until the mixture is damp enough to make a ball.

2 Sprinkle a little flour onto the work surface and roll the pastry out to a thickness of half a centimetre. Use a saucer to mark out the circles and cut them out with a knife.

3 Place the individual filling ingredients in a bowl. Mix them together well and add a sprinkling of salt and pepper.

4 Place the pastry circles on a greased baking tray. Place a large spoonful of filling in the middle of each pastry circle. Beat an egg in a bowl and brush a little on the edges of the pastry. Fold over the pastry to cover the filling. With the fork press down on the edges to seal the pastry parcel.

5 Use the pastry brush to paint egg over each finished pasty. Bake the pasties for 25 minutes at 180°C, 350°F, gas mark 4.

Always check with an adult before you use the kitchen.

Ask an adult to help when using the cooker.

Biscuits

For a special treat, home-made biscuits decorated with icing, silver balls cherries and sprinkles, will brighten up your tea time. Try both recipes (plain and chocolate), cut out in a variety of shapes with a mixture of patterns and designs, to create a colourful plateful of delicious biscuits. A few home-made biscuits in a decorative box or bag makes an ideal gift for parents or neighbours.

1 Use a wooden spoon to mix the flour, margarine (or butter), vanilla essence, sugar and baking powder until it looks like breadcrumbs. Add the egg and mix with a wooden spoon until it forms a dough.

2 Sprinkle a little flour onto the work surface and roll out the dough with a rolling pin. Do not press too hard. Dip the cutters in flour before cutting out a selection of shapes.

3 Place the biscuits on a greased baking tray. Bake for 15 minutes at 180°C, 350°F, gas mark 4. Allow to cool and decorate with icing, silver balls, cherries and sprinkles.

Ingredients

250g plain flour

125g margarine or butter

75g castor sugar

1 teaspoon baking powder

1 egg

For plain biscuits add:

1 teaspoon vanilla essence

For chocolate biscuits add:

25g cocoa powder

You will need:

Wooden spoon

Bowl

Biscuit cutters

Biscuit decorations

Ask an adult to help when using the cooker.

MILK, YOGHURT AND FRUIT
Dairy Drinks

Mix up milkshakes and smoothies in moments using one of these quick and easy recipes. Turn the kitchen into a milkbar and make drinks for the whole family. The smoothies are made from yoghurt and fresh fruit, cooled down with creamy ice cream and the milkshakes are made from fresh milk, ice cream and fruit. When you have tried these recipes maybe you would like to experiment with different flavours, fresh peaches and raspberry yoghurt, or maybe a banana and toffee ice cream milkshake! Remember to decorate your drinks with slices of fruit, whipped cream and paper parasols. Serve with long spoons.

You will need
Blender

Fresh fruit

Selection of ice creams

Milk

Yoghurt

Whipped cream

Straws

Decorations

Ask an adult to help when using the blender.

44

Strawberry milkshake

In the blender place 6 large strawberries, half a small banana, a scoop of strawberry ice cream and half a glass of milk. Blend well. Serve with whipped cream and sprinkle with hundreds and thousands on top.

Chocolate milkshake

In the blender place 1 small, roughly chopped banana, a large scoop of chocolate ice cream and half a glass of milk. Blend well. Serve with whipped cream, two or three banana slices and chocolate sprinkles on top.

Banana smoothie

In the blender place 1 roughly chopped banana, a scoop of vanilla ice cream and half a glass of natural yoghurt. Blend well and serve in a long glass.

Strawberry smoothie

In the blender place 6 large strawberries, a large scoop of strawberry ice cream and half a glass of strawberry yoghurt. Blend well and serve in a tall glass with a blob of strawberry yoghurt and a strawberry on top.

ICE CREAM
Sundaes

Have an ice cream sundae party for your friends. You will need a selection of ice creams, fresh fruit, custard, cream, jellies and decorative sprinkles. Try the home-made strawberry ice cream recipe, it is quick and easy to make. Fruit yoghurts can also be frozen and make tasty ice cream.

Always have an adult present when using sparklers or other fireworks.

Banana and chocolate ice cream sundae
Put one layer at a time into the glass. Start with some sliced banana, then add a spoonful of cold custard. Sprinkle on some chocolate flakes, then a small scoop of vanilla ice cream and decorate with heaps of whipped cream.

Strawberry trifle
Begin with a layer of crushed trifle biscuits. Mix 2 teaspoons of strawberry jam with 2 teaspoons of warm water and pour over the biscuits. Follow with custard then some chopped strawberries and jelly.
Finally decorate with whipped cream and a whole strawberry.

Sparkling ice cream sundae
Place a small tin of evaporated milk in the fridge for 2 hours. Pour the milk into a bowl and use a whisk to whip it until it is light and fluffy. Mix in the strawberries and syrup. Pour the mixture into a freezer-proof dish and freeze until solid. Serve it with a dazzling sparkler.

Bookmarks

Bookmarks will always come in handy, whether you enjoy fairytales or mysteries. These bookmarks are made from thin card and coloured with felt tip pens. A bookmark made from your initial written in bubble writing and decorated with bright colours would take no time to make. You could take inspiration from the book you are reading or make one representing a particular hobby or interest.

1 Use pencil to outline the whale. When you are happy with the shape cut it out.

Use felt tip pens to colour in the design and draw a neat border with a black felt tip pen.

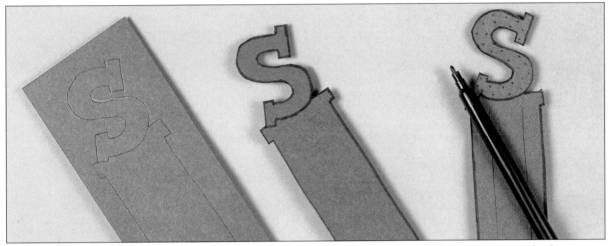

2 Personalise your bookmark by using your initial. Draw the outline in pencil first,

then go over it with a felt tip pen before you decorate the inner part of the initial.

3 This bookmark would look good in a gardening book!

You will need:
Thin card
Pencil
Scissors
Felt tip pens

TISSUE AND WIRE
Paper Flowers

S urprise a friend with a bunch of
scarlet poppies and fantasy flowers.
They are made from tissue paper and
florist's wire. The poppies are made up of
individual petals and look quite realistic
with their black-fringed stamens. The
fantasy flowers are easy to make from layers
of different colours – let your imagination
run riot and create a rainbow bouquet.

You will need:

Glue

Tissue paper in a variety of colours

Florist's wire

Green florist's tape

Scissors

1 Glue a scrunched-up piece of tissue paper onto one end of a piece of wire, for the centre of the poppy. Now glue the square of green paper over the poppy centre. Roll the black-fringed piece around the centre of the flower to make the stamens. Glue on the petals one at a time. Bend them slightly so they look realistic. Finally, use the green tape to tidy up the base of the flower and cover the wire.

2 Fantasy flowers are made from layers of coloured flower shapes. Begin by cutting the shape for the base or sepals of the flower. Layer three colours of tissue paper together, cut out a flower shape and then cut a small hole through the centre of the papers. Wind a small piece of paper around a wire to make the flower centre. Now use glue to attach the green sepal shape and the coloured flowers. Finally use the green tape to tidy up the base of the flower and cover the wire.

Making paper flowers takes practise. Don't expect the first one to come out perfectly, so keep trying. When you get a good shape make a bunch.

FELT
Beads

Turn ethnic-looking beads made from coloured felt into great chokers, bracelets and pendants. The beads are made from layers of felt glued or tied together. They are threaded on embroidery silk. Make a selection of colours and shapes and combine them with wooden beads to make an exotic necklace.

You will need:

Felt squares (from a craft shop)

Scissors

Fabric glue

Elastic band

Needle and coloured thread

Small quantity of stuffing

Ribbon

1. Cut three squares of coloured felt, each slightly smaller than the other. Layer them, using a little glue to hold them in place. Now roll them tightly in a sausage shape and hold in place with glue. You may need to wind a little thread around them or hold them in place with an elastic band. The glue will need to dry thoroughly. When the glue has set, use scissors to cut the sausage into beads.

2. You will need two squares of coloured felt. Cut out a heart shape from each colour, with one heart slightly smaller than the other. Place a little stuffing between the layers and sew them together with coloured thread. Make a ribbon loop at the top of the heart for threading.

3. Roll up a small square of felt. Hold the roll in place with glue. Wind coloured thread around the sausage-shaped felt pieces to make decorative bands.

Friendship Bracelets

Friendship bracelets are easier to make than you think, they just take a little time to practise. Choose several threads in strong or pastel colour combinations. Find a corner to settle down on your own where you can work without interruption and in time you will master the art and make a braid to wear and one to give to a special friend.

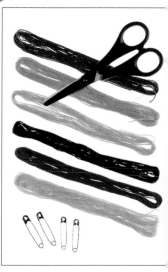

You will need:

Cork board or work surface

Selection of coloured thread

Sticky tape or safety pins

Scissors

1 You will need three lengths of thread. Make a knot to hold the threads together and attach the knot end to the board or worksurface with sticky tape or a safety pin.

2 Hold thread B with your left hand. Take thread A around B and push it through the loop to make a knot and pull the thread.

3 Repeat this action. You should have two knots on thread B.

4 Hold thread C with your left hand. Take thread A around C and through the loop to make a knot, pull the thread and then do it again. You should now have two knots on thread C. Thread A is now on the righthand side and you have completed the first row.

5 To start row two, make knots from left to right, knot B twice onto C, then twice onto A. For the third row, knot C twice onto A, then twice onto B.

6 Keep knotting the threads in rows until you have made a braid long enough to go round your wrist. Tie a firm knot to hold the loose ends in place.

7 Your friendship bracelet is now complete – make a double knot at each end and trim away any excess thread.

Remember to protect your work surface with newspaper or a vinyl cloth.

To make a wider braid use four, five or six threads. Make the braid as described above, knotting each thread twice, from left to right.

Candy Cushions

Dyed with wax crayons, these cushions will look soft and cuddly on your bed or on the playroom sofa. The cushions are made with calico fabric and are easy shapes to cut out and decorate. The wax crayon patterns can be ironed on to set them firmly. You could make a whole bag of candy cushions for your bed. A calico cat or doll would be great fun to decorate with wax crayons.

You will need:
Calico fabric

Wax crayons

Scissors

Needle and thread

Polyester stuffing

Brown paper

1 Fold the fabric in half to make a double layer. Draw on a large wrapped candy shape on the calico.

3 Cut out the cushion shapes and turn them right sides in. Sew together leaving a gap for the stuffing.

2 Use the wax crayons to colour the candy shape in swirls and dots, making it as realistic as possible.

4 Turn right side out. At this stage you should ask an adult to help iron the cushion shape between brown paper to seal the dye. Stuff the cushion with polyester.

Mobiles

Recycle milk and juice containers and turn them into colourful mobiles. The sleepy sheep would look good above your bed and the stars and flowers could hang in a sunny window. The mobiles are painted using water-soluble glass paints and outliners. If you don't have those to hand you can use coloured, permanent markers instead to create a similar effect.

You will need:

Florist's wire

Small pliers

Flat sided plastic milk or drink carton

Scissors

Outliner

Paint-brushes

Water-soluble glass paints

Needle

Gold thread

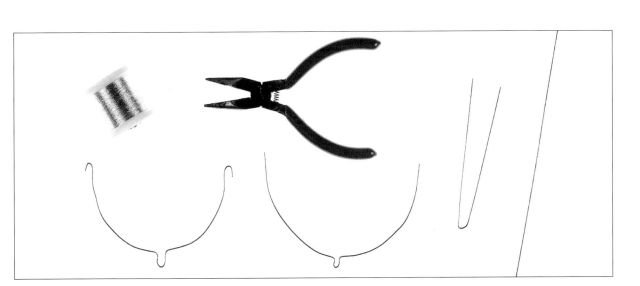

1 Florist's wire is easy to bend, start with a 20cm length. Begin by folding it in half. Then use the pliers to shape the mobile hanger and hooks. You will need three hangers for each mobile and each hanger should be exactly the same shape and size.

2 Use the scissors to cut the plastic container into suitable shapes for decoration. Wash the shapes and dry with a clean cloth. Outline the design and when the outliner is hard use a dry brush and glass paint to colour the shape.

3 Assemble the mobile by making a hole with the needle through the shapes and threading the gold thread through. Hang up the shapes and your mobile is complete.

Letter Rack

K eep your mail in check with these bright red tulips! The letter rack is made by slotting together thick flower patterns or maybe have a go at the ship at sea. The ship is a little more detailed, with the design cut from coloured paper.

1 Draw the design on thick, coloured card. The green bases will need to be cut straight to stand level on the table. The flowerheads are cut from coloured paper. Cut all the pieces out.

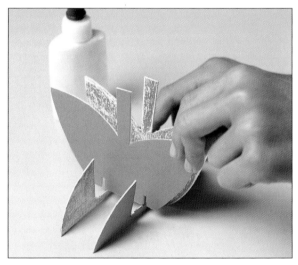

2 Colour the plain side of the card with crayons. Slot the letter rack together. You may need to make a rough one first to get the shape and slots right.

The letter rack can be made of card cut from a cereal packet or from a grocery box. You may need to cover the pieces of card with a layer of papier mâché to make them more sturdy and create a good surface to paint or colour.

3 Glue on the flower heads and your letter rack is ready to hold the mail.

You will need:

Thick coloured card

Scissors

Coloured paper

Crayons

Glue

Mirror Painting

Mirror, mirror on the wall who is the fairest of us all? Paint one of these pretty designs on a mirror tile to put up on the bathroom wall. The tiles are painted with glass paint which is available in a wide selection of colours and is very easy to use. The outliner divides the colours and comes in tubes that you use like a ball point pen, squeezing the colour gently onto the mirror.

You will need:

Mirror tiles or handbag mirrors

Glass paint outliners

Paper towel to mop up spills

Paint-brushes

Water-soluble glass paints

1 Use the outliner as if it were a pen, squeezing gently to allow a steady stream of the thick liquid onto the glass. Keep your paper towels handy in case of spills.

2 When the outliner is completely hard you can paint in the colour. Use a dry brush to dip into one colour at a time and wash and dry the brush well between colours.

Animal Pegs

Hold notes to your clipboard with a wild animal peg. The animals are drawn, cartoon-style, on thin card and coloured using felt tip pens. You could try gluing one of the finished pegs onto a magnet and attaching it to the fridge to hold notes. Practise your drawing on scrap paper first and look at comic strips and story book illustrations to get the style right.

You will need:
Thin card

Pencil

Scissors

Felt tip pens

Eraser

Glue

Pegs

Have a good look at these examples before you begin. Draw an outline with pencil. When you are happy with the shape, colour in the animal using felt tip pens. If you draw a dark outline around the coloured animal, you will see that this makes a big difference and gives the picture a professional finish. Cut out your animal and glue it onto a peg.

OVEN BAKE CLAY
Miniature Farm

This miniature farm can be made in an afternoon and could provide endless pleasure for a younger brother or sister. Stand it on a sunny windowsill to create a pretty country scene. Make a storage box for the farm from a matchbox covered with coloured paper and decorated in farmyard-style.

You will need:
Oven bake clay

Modelling tool and cocktail stick

Oven Tray

Match box

Coloured paper

Scissors

1 Begin by softening the white clay. Make the body first, then flatten a strip and fold it over the body as the ears. Now soften a small piece of black clay, and roll it into a sausage shape. Use the modelling tool to cut the legs and face.

2 These colourful hens are made from a small ball of brown clay. Press the clay to shape the head and tail of the hen. Make a base from a ball of green clay. Pinch out tiny pieces of red and yellow clay for the beak and comb.

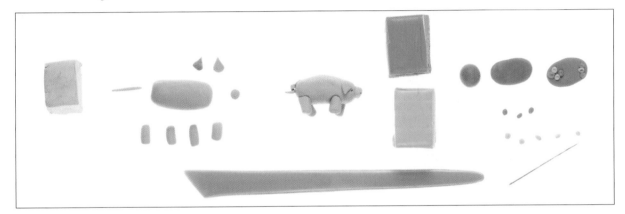

3 First soften the pink clay. Make a nice round sausage shape for the body. The pig's snout is made from a small flattened ball and its ears are made from flattened teardrop shapes. Roll out a smaller sausage shape and use the modelling tool to cut short legs. Roll out a thin tail and attach it firmly to the body.

To make some little patches of daisy-covered grass flatten an oval shape of green clay. Then make some small balls of yellow and green clay and use a cocktail stick or the tip of your modelling tool to lift them up and press them down onto the clay grass. When all your models are made, place them on a baking tray and harden them in the oven.

Follow the manufacturer's directions when baking the clay.

If you can't buy oven bake clay, you can use plasticine.

FABRIC
Scrunchies

Easy to make, you can have a scrunchy for every occasion. Sew them by hand in a running stitch or ask an adult to sew them for you, using a sewing machine. Thread them with elastic and decorate them imaginatively. Make scrunchies from ribbon, lace, velvet or dress fabric. A brightly coloured towelling scrunchy would be good for the seaside or swimming pool.

You will need:
Fabric and lace
Needle and thread or a sewing machine
Medium-sized safety pin
Half-centimetre wide elastic
Scissors
Sequins and glue

1 Lace: sew a centimetre-wide hem along one edge of the lace. Use the safety pin to thread the elastic through the seam. Tie the ends of the elastic into a knot and shape the scrunchy.

3 Tartan: this attractive scrunchy is made in the same way as the velvet scrunchy. Use matching thread to sew the seams.

2 Velvet: fold the fabric in half lengthways, with the wrong side out. Sew a seam. Turn the velvet tube the right way round by pulling one end through the other. Sew a channel in matching thread along one side and thread the elastic through.

4 Sequin: make this party time scrunchy in the same way as the tartan and velvet scrunchies. Decorate it with shiny sequins glued or sewn onto the fabric.

Gift Boxes

Surprise your friends with one of these stylish hand made boxes. Make small boxes from paper or slightly larger boxes from thin card. A double layer of wrapping paper would make an attractive box. Use paper that suits the gift and make a box from flowery paper to hold packets of seeds or use red paper for a Valentine box. Plain paper can be decorated with stickers or coloured tape. Try decorating paper first with crayons or pencils. A set of boxes could be used to hold cake and party favours and you could personalize the boxes with your guests' names. Once you have mastered the method you will find the boxes quick and easy to make.

You will need:
Paper

Ruler

Scissors

Glue

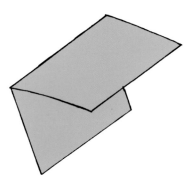

1 Fold a rectangular piece of paper in half.

2 Fold each half in on itself, so that both ends meet in the middle.

3 With the paper opened out, you will see crease marks like this.

4 Now fold the paper into thirds in the opposite direction to your first folds.

5 Now the creases should look like this.

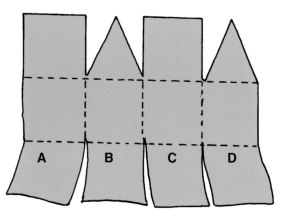

A   B   C   D

6 Cut along the crease lines and cut out the triangles as shown in the picture above.

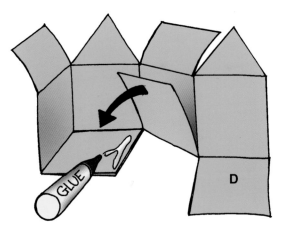

GLUE

D

7 Fold in and glue flap B onto flap A, flap C onto flap B and flap D onto flap C. Finally stick the open edge with sticky tape on the inside and make a hole at the top of both triangles for a ribbon.

Pop-up Cards

This pop-up card is simple to make and will brighten up someone's day. When placed on a windowsill or mantlepiece it will look as if a bunch of flowers is bursting out of the card. The cards are made and decorated with thin card. If you don't have any coloured thin card available, use card from a cereal packet and paint it in bright colours yourself.

You will need:

Coloured thin card

Scissors

Glue

Coloured paper

Felt tips pens

1 Begin by folding a sheet of thin card in half and then open it out. Cut out a small square of card and fold it in half. Fold a lip on the two edges, and glue these into the card to make the vase. Open and close the card to check the vase flattens when you close it.

2 Using green thin card, cut the stalks and leaves, use glue to attach these to the inside of the vase. Cut out some tulip-shaped flowers and glue them onto the stalks, making sure that they are hidden when the card is closed.

3 Cut small heart shapes to decorate the vase from red paper, folded over.

4 Now decorate the front of the card with a large red heart and a smaller blue heart, to match the rest of the design. Now you are ready to write your message on the card, using felt tip pens.

When trying out something for the first time, start by making a rough example out of scrap paper and card.

Bows & Ribbons

Bows and ribbons provide the final touch to a beautifully wrapped gift. You can decorate plain ribbon with felt tip pens, creating your own designs. The ribbons shown here are decorated with tiny motor vehicles and balloons, but any design would be fun. Hallowe'en pumpkins or Christmas trees are bright and easy to draw. Bows are quick to make using the method shown. Choose thin ribbon to make small bows and wider ribbon for larger bows. Co-ordinate the patterns and colours of your home made bows with wrapping paper for a stylish look.

You will need:

Ribbon

Felt tip pens

Ruler

Scissors

Needle and thread

1 Use felt tip pens to decorate plain ribbon. Cut a little ribbon off to practise on. Press the pen down gently to prevent the colour bleeding across the weave of the ribbon.

Complete the use of one colour before moving on to the next. Remember to repeat your pattern to give the ribbon a shop bought look.

2 Spread a 60cm length of ribbon across the work surface. Use a felt tip pen and ruler to make a tiny mark every 6cm. Thread the needle with thread about 20cm longer than the ribbon and make a good knot at the end. Sew a small stitch at each mark on the ribbon. Now pull gently at the thread and the ribbon should bunch up, making a fancy bow.

Printed Cards

S pend a rainy afternoon making potato cuts to print with and you will be able to set up a production line and make a collection of cards or writing paper. The fish card is made with layers of different coloured paper, each slightly smaller than the other. Biscuit cutters come in lots of shapes and provide a quick way to make home made stamps. Use a small rabbit shape to decorate writing paper and envelopes. The bunch of carrots is made by first drawing the shape onto the potato half, then cutting it out with a knife. A set of cards tied with matching ribbon would make a good gift.

You will need:

A potato

Biscuit cutters

Knife

Paint and saucer

Sponge

Paper

1 Begin by cutting a potato in half. Take the fish-shaped biscuit cutter and press it firmly into the flesh of one half of the potato. Use the knife to cut around the shape. Lift off the cutter and remove the excess potato flesh. Put a little paint onto a saucer and use the sponge to evenly distribute the paint on the stamp. Now press the stamp gently onto blue paper. Print a few fish and leave them to dry.

2 Take a white sheet of paper and fold it in half to make the card. Now take a square of blue paper slightly smaller than the card and glue it on the front. Next glue on a small piece of gold paper. Cut out the fish print and glue it on top.

3 To finish off the picture you will need to make a simple stamp from the other half of the potato. Use the knife to cut a weed shape. Spread green paint on the stamp and print leaves of sea weed onto the card. Leave to dry.

Protect your work surface with newspaper or a plastic cloth before you begin.

It is a good idea to practise stamping your design on some scrap paper to get an idea of how much paint you need to apply to the stamp.

Concertina Cards

Make one of these cards and watch the concertina movement when you open and close the card. The clown gives a good impression of playing his concertina, and the ballerina's tutu stands proudly out. The poodle's ruff looks almost real! The cards are quite simple to make, so think up some ideas of your own. You could use the concertina shape to make a bumble bee's body, or maybe a wriggly worm holding an umbrella! Use a little imagination and some brightly coloured paper to create a novel concertina card for a friend's birthday.

1 Fold a sheet of paper in half to form the card. Use the ruler to measure where to fix the concertina ends. Mark the two points, which should be evenly spaced on either side of the central fold.

2 Draw the clown with the arms ending at the dots. Make the picture quite simple.

3 Colour in your picture with bright shades, making it as attractive as possible.

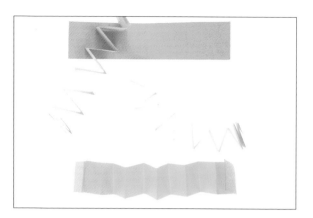

4 You will need to cut a long narrow strip of yellow paper to make the concertina. Fold it to form a fan. When folding paper always use your thumbnail to press the fold firmly down.

5 Use glue to attach each end of the concertina to the end of the clown's arms.

You will need:

Paper

Ruler

Felt tip pens

Scissors

Glue

Gift Bags

Pack your Christmas gifts in these brightly coloured paper bags. You can make them almost any size. Use one layer of paper for smaller bags and a double layer to make larger bags. You could decorate the paper before you begin. Make a stencil to decorate the paper if you are making a lot of bags all to match for party favours. The bag handles can be made from string or pretty ribbon. Have a look around for paper decorated on both sides, or use gold or silver paper.

You will need:

A selection of paper

Glue

Hole punch

Ribbon

1 Begin by folding the paper in by about one quarter of its length. Run your thumbnail along the fold to mark it well.

2 Turn the folded sheet of paper over and apply glue to one end.

3 Glue the edges together to form a cylinder shape. Allow the glue to dry.

4 Flatten the cylinder shape. Run your thumbnail along the edges to make a good fold.

5 Fold about one quarter over on each side.

6 Open the two folds and press them inwards. You should now have a bag shape.

7 Make a fold upwards to form the base of the bag. Glue it down.

8 Use a hole punch to make holes to thread a ribbon through and make a handle.

Cut-out Cards

Make a row of paper flowerpots and turn them into a birthday card, or a row of blue and white teapots to send as an invitation to tea. The Christmas tree cards can be decorated as brightly as you wish and the colourful fish swimming around in their bowls will brighten up the mantlepiece. Cut-out cards are quick and easy to make and decorate. When choosing the shape remember that the card will need to be cut out so draw a compact picture. A Christmas tree cut from plain white paper and decorated using a gold pen would be very stylish.

You will need:

Paper

Felt tip pens

Crayons

Scissors

Glue

Sequins to decorate

When decorating your cards try outlining coloured-in pictures with a darker shade. This will accentuate the shapes and give the cards a professional finish.

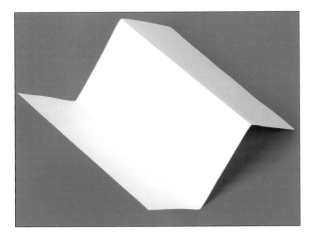

1 This card is easy to make and fun to colour, you will need a rectangle of plain white paper. Fold the sheet of paper in three to make the card shape

2 On the front of the card draw a pot of flowers. Make sure the flower pots are joined at the lip, or the card will fall apart when you cut it out.

3 Cut away the excess paper.

4 Colour in your card using bright shades.

5 To make this cheery Christmas card use a sheet of green paper folded in three. Draw on the Christmas tree shape and cut it out. Take care to leave the branches joined together at the base of the tree. Glue on small flowerpots cut from paper for the trees to stand in and decorate the Christmas trees with sequins and shiny stars, glued on.

Stained Glass

Create your own stained glass pictures with coloured plastic wrapping. Placed where the light shines through them these cards are most effective. Coloured wrapping film is available from craft shops, however you might want to save sweet wrappers and keep an eye out for coloured clear plastic to recycle. The holly leaves make a good Christmas card. You can have fun decorating the card with coloured glitter glue.

You will need:

Black paper

Felt tip pen

Scissors

Coloured clear wrapping

Glue and glitter glue

1 To make this clear blue fish bowl card begin by folding a sheet of white paper in half. Draw on a simple fish bowl shape and cut it out.

3 Use glitter glue to fill the bowl with fish, coloured seaweed and pebbles. Don't forget to paint on air bubbles. Decorate the edge of the bowl as well.

2 Cut a rectangle of blue coloured wrapping slightly larger than the fish bowl. Glue the rectangle onto the inside of the card, covering the fish bowl shape. Fold the card closed. You will decorate the cover of the card.

4 You will need a sheet of black paper folded in half to make the holly card. Begin by cutting out the holly leaves and berries. Cut green coloured wrapping slightly larger than the cut-out leaves and glue it to the inside of the card. Use red wrapping for the berries. Fold the card to close it and decorate the stained glass-effect card with coloured glitter glue.

If you do not have glitter glue, make your own. Use PVA glue and mix in an equal amount of fine glitter. Use a fine paint-brush to apply the glitter glue to your model or card.

TISSUE PAPER

Stencilled Wrapping Paper

Stencilling is a quick and effective way to decorate wrapping paper and gift tags. Use gold or silver paint to turn plain tissue paper into expensive looking wrapping paper. The stencils are easily cut from small sheets of paper folded in half. You could make matching gift wrap and tags to suit any event or gift. Once you have mastered the art of stencilling you may want to try using two colours. It is also useful to remember that other colouring materials and methods are good for stencilling. You don't have to use paint, try wax crayons for example.

You will need:

Paper

Pencil

Scissors

Tissue paper

Paint

Saucer

Sponge

Hole punch

Thread

Always protect your work surface with newspaper or a vinyl cloth.

Remember to wipe up any spills as they happen. A good craftsperson leaves a tidy work surface.

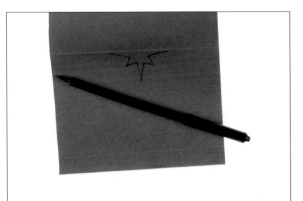

1 To make a stencil you will need a small sheet of paper. Fold it in half and draw on half of the picture, in this case half of the star, as shown in the picture above.

2 Use the scissors to cut the star out, taking care not to leave any jagged edges and not to cut into the paper. If you do, the stencil paint may come through.

3 Spread a sheet of tissue paper across your work surface. Pour a little paint onto the saucer, spread it on the sponge, damping the sponge down. Place the stencil on some rough paper and practise until you are confident.

4 Stencil on the stars taking care not to smudge the paint when you lift the stencil off the paper. Hang your stencilled paper up to dry. It is a good idea to make quite a few sheets at a time, as well as matching gift tags.

5 Use paper to make these matching gift tags. Cut them out with scissors. Stencil on the star and leave to dry.

6 Use a hole punch to make a hole for the thread to tie the tag onto the gift.

Tissue Paper Cards

Tissue paper comes in such a wide range of colours, it is easy to tear and sticks with the minimum of glue. When decorating cards there is no end to the number of ways you can use tissue paper. These cards are made from torn strips of tissue and layered to create blended colours and a simple design. The colours are bright and breezy and very stylish. Have a go at layering colours yourself. Create a natural looking landscape with torn or cut greens, blues and browns.

You will need:

Coloured paper

Tissue paper

Scissors

Glue

1 Fold a piece of coloured paper in half to form the card. Tear off pieces of lime green tissue paper and use small amounts of glue to stick them onto the card.

3 This eyecatching Valentine card is easy to make. You will need to layer 4 pieces of red tissue paper together, fold them in half and carefully tear out a heart shape. The border of the card is made from scissor-cut pieces of red tissue paper.

2 Now layer on strips of pink tissue paper and follow these with a border of blue tissue paper strips. When the glue has set, your card is ready for you to sign and send to a friend.

DRIFTWOOD
Boats

When you go for a walk along the beach keep your eyes open for unusual items. This is called beachcombing. Driftwood is often washed up on the shore and collecting it is great fun, but what can you do with all those oddly shaped pieces of wood? Making small boats is one way of using them. The sails and flags can be cut from coloured tissue paper. You could make a miniature fleet of small craft and feature them on a sunny windowsill. You will need your imagination to create interesting boats, masts and sails. If you want to join pieces together, you will need to use a strong glue. Driftwood often looks good left a natural colour. However it sometimes needs decorating.

You will need:

Selection of driftwood pieces

Tissue paper

Sturdy scissors

Glue

Tissue paper

Paint

Paint-brush

Emery board

1 When making driftwood boats spend a lot of time planning the best use of particular pieces of wood you may have found. Occasionally you will find one that needs just a sail or a dot of paint to turn it into an interesting craft.

Sometimes you will need to change the shape of a piece of wood; strong scissors may do. Try using an emery board or a small piece of sandpaper to shape pieces to fit neatly together. Most of all you need to enjoy being creative with your seaside materials.

When beachcombing take care you do not injure yourself. Wear beachshoes and use rubber gloves. Check found items for nails and do not touch anything you don't recognize.

SHELLS AND DRIFTWOOD
Mobiles

Beachcombing can be very rewarding: the tides wash all sorts of things up on the beach. Interesting pieces of water-smoothed driftwood and pretty shells can be turned into mobiles and hung up as a reminder of seaside days. When making a mobile you need a shapely piece of driftwood to start with. You can use thread or string to tie on attractive shells and stones. The mobile needs to be well balanced. Check this by hanging the mobile up as soon as you have a few pieces tied on, adjusting the weight as you go. Paint on a layer of varnish for a glossy look.

You will need:

Driftwood	Shells
Pebbles	Thread
Small nails	Paint-brush
Scissors	Varnish

1 You will need a piece of driftwood and some small nails to make the hanger for this mobile. Use a hammer to knock the nails into position.

2 Tie good knots when attaching the shells and driftwood to the string. Consider how the mobile will appear when hung up when you do this.

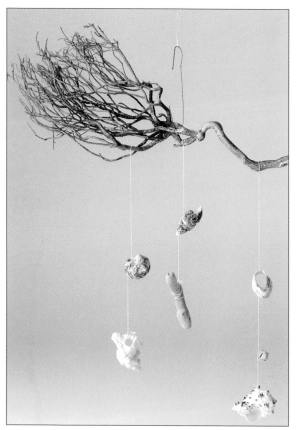

4 This mobile is made by tying the weighted strings directly onto the driftwood. You could use loops and hang the strings on or tie them on with small tight knots. You will need to check the mobile for balance as you make it. When the mobile is complete you might want to paint on a layer of varnish to give the shells a glossy finish.

3 Once you are happy with the balance of the mobile, paint a layer of varnish onto the shells. Hang up your mobile and let it remind you of a very happy holiday.

Paperweights

Pebble painting is fun and a good rainy day activity. Collect pebbles along the beach and save them. When you want to enjoy a quiet time get out the paints and your imagination, and make these attractive paperweights. You could paint a tiny row of pebble cottages (use a fine paint-brush to paint on tiny windows and doors) and little rose bushes along the cottage front. Or try your hand at painting a tiny kitten on a pebble or a fish or even a skeleton.

1 These interesting decorations need a little time and practice. Wash and dry the pebbles before you begin. Use a fine paint-brush to paint in the detail. Once you are happy with your chosen decoration and the paint has dried, add a layer of varnish.

2 A row of painted pebble cottages makes a good ornamental display. Choose pebbles which have suitable shapes and which can stand up. You may need to apply two coats of paint to the house and roof to give a good surface for decorating. When you have painted the cottages give them a coat of varnish to protect them and to give them a glossy finish.

You will need:
Pebbles
Paint, varnish and paint-brushes

Lighthouse

Models are great fun to make. This lighthouse standing on a rocky island surrounded by the blue sea looks very realistic. Spend some time planning your model, then make a rough drawing. If you have been to the seaside you may recall a particular lighthouse or other seaside scene which you could re-create in miniature. When you are away on holiday you may want to collect a few pebbles and some sand to use to make the model when you return home. It is amazing what you can achieve with some plaster, pebbles and paint.

You will need:

A cardboard lid

Margarine tub

Stones

Pebbles

Plaster-of-Paris

Bowl and spatula

Air hardening clay

Glue

Paint and paint-brushes

1 Place the margarine tub towards one end of the box lid. Position the stones; they will jut out of the 'water' so need to be quite tall. When you are happy with the arrangement mix up the plaster-of-Paris in the bowl and pour it over everything.

2 You will now need to make the lighthouse. Use some air hardening clay and make a long cylinder shape, wider at one end than the other. The room at the top will need to be made separately. Leave the pieces to dry in a warm airy spot.

3 When the plaster and the lighthouse pieces are dry you can glue everything in place. Use strong glue. Leave the model in a warm airy spot to dry.

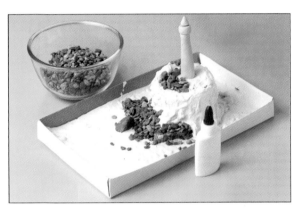

4 Spread a thick layer of glue where ever you need to place the small pebbles. These will give the impression of rocks. A few on top of the island will look good.

5 Once your model is dry it is ready to paint and decorate. Have fun and use plenty of imagination to create a realistic-looking rocky, seaside scene.

Photo Album

Seaside holidays are best remembered in photographs. Make one of these albums to keep your photographs safe. Choose bright nautical colours; blue and yellow are fun. The albums are made from card and coloured cord holds the pages together. Try making a seaside collage to decorate the cover. A beach scene or a gaily coloured yacht would look good.

You will need:

Thin coloured card

Coloured paper

Scissors

Hole punch

Cord

1 Cut the covers and pages to size. Use the hole punch to make holes through the covers and pages. You will need to take care that they line up. Thread coloured cord through the holes to hold the album together securely and tie a bow.

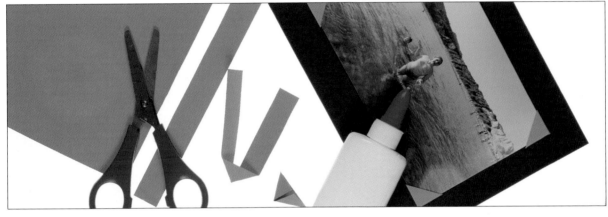

2 To make the photograph holders cut a narrow strip of paper. Fold the paper inwards to create a corner sleeve. Cut away any excess paper and glue the sleeve onto the page. Do this four times, one for each corner then insert the photograph.

3 Decorate the cover of your album with an attractive seaside collage. Use coloured paper to create this yacht and cut out a row of waves to glue along the bottom of the page.

Seaside Jewellery

Shells, attractive stones and small pieces of driftwood can be made up into earrings and pendants. Use fine wire and thread to assemble the jewellery. You can also buy ready-made clasps and earring backs from craft shops. These are called jewellery findings. Look along the seashore for two matching shells with small holes in and make them up into earrings. As you walk along the beach keep an eye out for interestingly shaped, coloured stones.

You will need:

Pebbles and shells

Wire

Thread

Jewellery findings

Varnish

Paint-brush

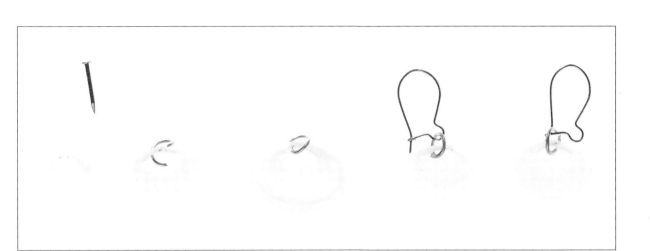

1 These dainty shell earrings are easy to make. These shells have tiny holes naturally occurring in them. However you may have to use a press–together jewellery binding to hold the shell in place. Attach the earring hook to each shell and you have a pretty pair of earrings to wear as a reminder of your seaside visit.

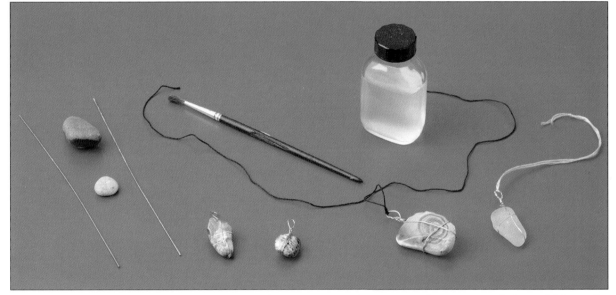

2 To make these pendants you will need some attractively marked pebbles. Use clear varnish painted over the pebbles to bring out the rich patterns (clear nail varnish works just as well).

Wind a piece of wire around the pebble and finish with a loop at the top. Attach a piece of thread to the loop and use this to hang your pendant around your neck.

Check that it is okay to pick up shells along the beach where you are.

Three-in-a-row

Three-in-a-row is a good game to both make and to play. Once you have made a board you can make a selection of counters, different sets to suit different occasions. The boards are made from card and craft wood while the counters are made from oven bake clay.

Matching shells make good counters too. To play the game you need two players. Each player takes turns placing a counter on the board. You must both try to take defensive action when it's your turn, to prevent the other player from getting three-in-a-row. The first player to get a row wins.

You will need:

Thick coloured card

Craft strip-wood

Scissors

Paint-brush

Oven bake clay

Shells

Glue

1 Begin by painting the craft strip-wood in your chosen colour. Choose a colour that co-ordinates with the thick coloured card you will use for the base of the board. Leave it until it is thoroughly dry.

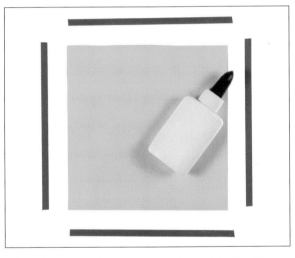

2 The size of your games board is decided by the piece of thick coloured card. This will need to be square. Cut the sides for your board to length from the craft strip-wood, using your board as a pattern.

3 Attach the sides to the board with glue. Cut the board markings from thin strip-wood and glue these in place. Make sure you position them correctly on the board.

4 Glue on the cross markings. Don't worry if your paintwork gets a little scratched. Once the glue is dry you can use paint to touch up any spots that might need it.

5 These noughts and crosses counters are made from oven bake clay. Use different colours and check that the counters fit the available space on the board. Try your hand at making little boats, dolphins and starfish as a variation from flat counters.

MOSAIC
Tablemats

Mosaics are usually created using small square tiles. To make these tablemats we have cut lots of small squares from paper and used them glued onto sugar paper to create a fishy picture. Choose bright colours to create your pictures. Squares cut from magazine pictures can also be used to make mosaics. The important thing to remember, when making a mosaic, is to keep the lines straight. This gives the impression of tiles all lined up. Use a ruler and pencil to make markings on your paper so that you can keep the squares neat and in order.

You will need:
Paper
Ruler
Pencil
Scissors
Glue

1 Begin by drawing a simple outline of a fish on your paper. Make sure that the picture is centrally placed.

4 Your finished fish mosaic should look something like this. You could make a set of table mats for the family.

2 Use the ruler and pencil to measure out squares and cut them out in your chosen colours. You will need a lot of squares.

5 For a special event you might want to decorate some table napkins to match your table mats. Use paper and create pretty collage pictures.

3 Glue on the squares. Begin in a corner of the picture and try to work from one side of the picture to the other.

CARD AND GLITTER
Aquarium

The fish floating in this model aquarium are made from thin card and decorated with paint and glitter. They shimmer through the weed and clear blue sea very realistically when you gently shake the box. Use a large shoe box to make the aquarium. You could make a shoal of tiny fish to weave their way through the weed. The fish are suspended from the ceiling of the box with thin gold thread which is almost invisible. Place a few rocks and shells in the bottom of the box. If you have one, a model shipwreck would make an attractive feature.

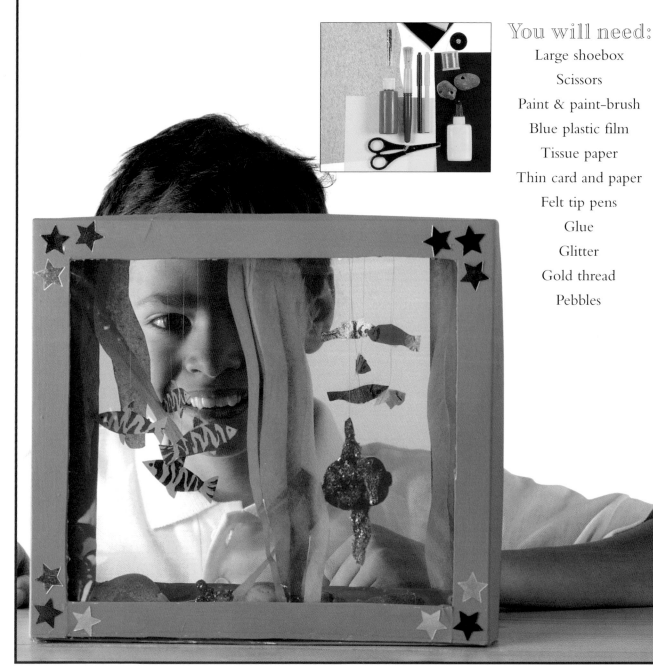

You will need:

Large shoebox

Scissors

Paint & paint-brush

Blue plastic film

Tissue paper

Thin card and paper

Felt tip pens

Glue

Glitter

Gold thread

Pebbles

1 Cut a rectangle from the box lid.

2 Cut a rectangle from the base of the box.

3 Paint the box and lid blue, inside and out.

4 Glue blue film over the cut-out spaces.

5 Cut strips of tissue paper for weeds. Glue them in place suspended from the roof of the aquarium. Use two colours of green.

6 Draw fish on the thin card and decorate them with paint and glitter. Attach them to the lid of the box with gold thread.

Fishing Game

Fishing games always go down well at parties and games evenings. This fishing game is quite easy to make. The fish hooks and the fish mouths are made from paper clips. You could also make fish in two colours or make several different sea creatures, such as fish and starfish. Then players can see how many of each they can 'catch' in a given time. Another game might be to give each fish a value, adding the values at the end of the game to see which 'catch' is worth the most. This would introduce gamesmanship as each player goes for the highest value catch.

You will need:

Plate

Thick card

Thin card

Scissors

Glue

Sticky tape

Ruler

Felt tips

Sticks

String

Paper clips

1 Use a plate as an outline for a circular shape on a piece of thick card. Cut out the circle. This will be the base of the pond. Measure out a long strip of thin card for the sides. Tape it to the base.

4 Now make the loops on the decorated stars and fish from paper clips. You will need to fold up a section of the paper clip and attach it with sticky tape to the fish and starfish.

2 The sides of the pond will prevent the fish from jumping out! Use coloured tape or felt tip pens to decorate the sides.

5 The fishing rods are made from garden sticks. Tie a piece of string to one end of each stick and a paper clip to the end of each piece of string. Shape the paper clip into a hook

3 Draw the fish and starfish on a piece of thick card and decorate them using felt tip pens. Cut them out. You will need to make quite a few fish and starfish.

SEASHELL

Treasure Boxes

hells can be used decoratively in so many ways. In this project they are used to decorate a small storage box and to make a pretty circular picture frame. You will need an empty cheese box and some shells to make the storage box plus some grout or strong glue to attach the shells. You can arrange them in a regular pattern or randomly over the lid. The picture frame is made from thin card.

You will need:

Empty cheese box

Selection of shells

Grout

Spatula

Thin card

Scissors

Varnish

Paint-brush

If you do not have any grout you could use some strong glue.

1 First check that the box is clean. Before you begin, experiment with the design. Lay the shells on the lid without any grout. When you are happy with the design spread a layer of grout across the box lid using the spatula and gently press the shells in place.

3 To make this pretty shell encrusted picture frame you will need a circle of thin card with a hole cut out of the centre. This will make the frame shape. Apply a layer of grout using the spatula and gently press the shells into an attractive pattern around the edge.

2 Leave the box in a warm airy spot to dry. You will need to give the shell covered box plenty of time to dry off. When it is dry paint on a layer of varnish to give the shells an attractive finish.

4 When the grout has dried the frame is ready for a layer of varnish. This will protect it and bring out the colours. Now you can insert a photograph and hang up the frame or use it as a small paperweight.

BOTTLE TOPS
Snake

This beautiful sinuous snake can be made from bottle tops. You will need to collect a lot of bottle tops, so it may be worth asking friends to save them for you. By combining different coloured tops you could create a multi-coloured snake and if you saved only one colour of bottle tops your snake would still be dramatic. The silver shimmers and the closely fitted bottle tops give the appearance of scales when wriggled along the floor. The snake's head is made from a cork and his bright red tongue is a piece of felt, cut to shape and pushed into the cork.

You will need:

Hammer

Large nail

Piece of wood

Bottle tops

Strong string

Scissors

Cork

Glue

Paint & paint-brushes

Small piece of felt

1 Hammer a nail through a piece of wood near its end. You can then hold the wood and position the nail to make the hole in the centre of the bottle top.

When all the bottle tops have holes in them thread them onto the string. Think about your colour co-ordination. A snake like this one will need approximately 70 bottle tops.

2 Attach a piece of cork to each end of the string of bottle tops. One end will be the tail – paint it green. The other end will be the head – paint this green as well and add two spots for the eyes. Cut a small piece of felt into the shape of a snake's tongue and press it into the cork with the point of the nail.

Pocket Pets

These cute little pets don't need feeding or cleaning out, just a little loving! The animals are made from oven bake clay, simply shaped and pressed together. Give the dog big soppy eyes by using a white flattened ball and laying a black eyespot on top of it. Place the black eyespot carefully as that is what gives them character.

The dog collar is another important item. Be sure to give your pets a tag with your telephone number on it in case they wander off! Make a water bowl and bone – and maybe a few doggy toys would be a good idea. The kennels are made from recycled milk or juice cartons. Paint them in bright colours and write your pet's name above the entrance.

You will need:

Oven bake clay

Modelling tool

Empty milk or juice carton

Scissors

Paint

Paint-brush

Large flat lid for
the cat's basket

1 To make the dog, soften the clay between your fingers then shape the body and feet. Take a small piece of dark brown clay and roll out a thin tail. Make a flattened sausage shape for the ears and lastly make the eyes and collar. Assemble your little pet and bake it in the oven according to the manufacturer's instructions.

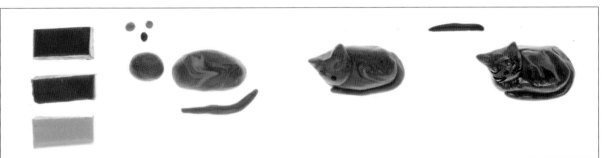

2 To make the cat you will need orange, yellow and brown clay. Roughly mix equal quantities of orange and yellow clay. Shape the body first and then the head. Use your fingertips to pinch out the ears. Roll out thin pieces of brown clay to make the cat's whiskers and eyes and position them on the face. When you are happy with the shape of your pet, bake it in the oven according to the manufacturer's instructions.

3 To make this roomy kennel you will need an empty milk or juice carton. Cut out the shape and mark the entrance. Paint the kennel in attractive colours. You might want to write your pet's name above the entrance hole.

If you don't have any oven bake clay make your pets from Plasticine.

PLASTIC CONTAINERS AND OVEN BAKE CLAY
Skittles

Enjoy a game of skittles whenever you like with these brightly decorated recycled drink containers. You will need six containers to make a set. Paint them in bright colours and decorate them with coloured stars. If they get knocked over too easily, pour some sand into each one to make them heavier. Mini- or table-skittles can also be fun. You could make a set to take away on holiday. They are made from oven bake clay. Take turns with a friend to see how many skittles you can knock down with each shot.

You will need:
Empty drink containers

Paint

Paint-brushes

Sand, for weight

To make mini-skittles you will need:

Oven bake clay

1 Wash out the drink containers well. Leave upside down to drain. Screw the lids on tightly and your skittles are ready for painting. Begin by painting a base coat.

You may need two layers of paint. When the base coat is dry, paint on the decoration. When all your skittles are painted and decorated they are ready for use.

2 To make these mini-skittles you will need oven bake clay in three colours. Divide the clay into equal pieces and shape the skittles. Use oven bake clay of a different colour to make flattened ball shapes and press them onto the skittles. Shape a ball and when your ball and skittles are ready, bake in the oven according to the manufacturer's directions. You might want to decorate a small box in which to store your mini-skittles.

A set of mini-skittles would make a good Christmas cracker gift or party favour.

A full size set of skittles could be used at a school games day or fund raising event.

PLASTIC AND PAPER

Magic Pictures

This fishy picture changes from black and white to colour quite magically. Make one to delight a younger brother or sister. Choose your picture carefully: an empty black and white hillside could turn into a green pasture covered with sheep, or a bare table top could have a birthday cake appear on it.

Use brightly coloured felt tip pens to colour your picture. It is a good idea to keep the shapes simple. If you don't have a plastic folder you might be able to recycle a piece of clear plastic from a carton.

You will need:
Thin card or paper

Scissors

Marker and felt tip pens

Plastic folder

Sticky tape

1 Take a sheet of thin card or paper and fold it carefully into three equal sections as shown in the picture.

2 On the front flap mark out a rectangle and the finger grip space. Cut away the finger grip space.

3 Open out the card and cut out the rectangle. This is the front of the card.

4 Draw a decorative border on this front frame. Cut a separate piece of paper the same size as one section of the card and draw on your design, using felt tip pens.

5 Slip your picture into the plastic folder with the top against a fold. Trim the plastic to the picture. Stick the back to the plastic.

6 Use a marker pen to draw an outline of the picture on the plastic. Now take your card and open it out flat.

7 Fold the bottom flap into the middle. Slip the plastic-covered picture over the bottom flap. The bottom flap is now between the coloured picture and the outlined picture on the plastic flap. Fold the top flap down over the plastic. Grip the plastic and paper and pull; the picture will appear in colour as you pull it out.

Doll's House

Make a cute little doll's house for a miniature doll or bear to live in. This house is made from two boxes. Use any card you may have over to make miniature furniture. You may want to have a look round for some small matchboxes or other containers to recycle as furniture. Coloured paper makes good wallpaper, as does wrapping paper. Use a piece of fabric to make carpets and rugs, and don't forget some pictures to go on the walls. Decorate the outside of your house with paint, creating a cheerful summery scene for your doll to live in.

You will need:

Two shoeboxes

Scissors

Tape & glue

Large paper clips

Paint & paint-brushes

Paper & card

Small boxes

Felt tip pens

1 Use one of the boxes to make the house. Cut a corner off the other box to make the roof and cut the lid so that it fits inside the house as the upstairs floor.

2 Place the shoe box that will be the house up on one end. Use tape to attach the roof piece you have prepared at an angle to the top of the house. Use glue and tape to stick the floor section into place. Hold the floor in position with the large paperclips while the glue is setting.

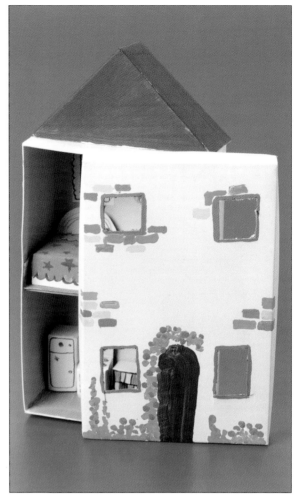

3 When the glue is set your house is ready to decorate. Paint the roof a rich reddy brown and the walls pale pink. Make a front for the house from the other shoe-box lid and cut out windows. Paint a bright front door and flowers and make your house summery and cheerful.

4 Miniature furniture is easy to make from scraps of paper and small boxes. Cover boxes with white paper to make kitchen equipment and coloured paper for furniture in other rooms. Use felt tip pens to outline shapes and decorate the pieces. Don't forget wallpaper and rugs and maybe some pictures on the walls.

CARDBOARD
Toy Cars

These cute little cars are great fun to make and given a push will whizz along a smooth surface. The wheels are made from milk or juice container lids, cocktail sticks and straws. The car chassis is cut from either coloured card or the sides of a recycled grocery box.

You will need:

Thick card

Scissors

Masking tape

Paint

Paint-brushes

Four juice or milk carton lids

Straws

Cocktail sticks

1 Begin by drawing two side views of a car. Cut them out. Next cut out a long rectangular shape. The width of the rectangle decides how wide the car is.

2 Use the scissors to cut out two small v-shapes to form the wheel arches. The wheel axles will run through these v-shapes. The wheel axles will be held in place by the base of the car.

3 Now you are ready to assemble your car. Use masking tape to attach the long rectangular shape to the car sides. Do this and you will see the car take shape.

4 Cut a piece of card to fit in the base of the car. Tape it in place. Your car is now ready to paint and decorate. You could paint on a family sitting in the car.

5 To make the wheels each lid will need a hole made through its centre. Push the end of a straw through the hole. Now use a cocktail stick to hold it in place. Break the ends off so that the wheel turns.

6 Push the wheel axle all the way through and attach the second wheel. Cut off any long pieces of straw to fit the car. Now make and fit the second axle.

GREEN LENTILS AND FABRIC

Juggling Balls

Juggling is a great skill to develop. It takes time and patience but can be most fulfilling. Make yourself some juggling balls and a set for a friend and practise together. These juggling balls are made from printed cotton fabric and filled with uncooked green lentils. Lentils are a perfect filling as they will give the juggling balls some weight and be easy to grip. They are also quite economically priced – and – if you stop juggling you can cook the lentils for supper!

1 Cut a rectangle of fabric and fold it in half. Sew seams along the side edges. Sew strong stitches close together or ask an adult for help and use a sewing machine.

4 Close the bag making a triangular shape by bringing the two side seam ends together and neatly fold the edges inside to allow for the final seam.

2 Turn the bag shape right side out.

5 Sew the edge together firmly.

3 Half fill the bags with green lentils.

Juggling balls would make a great birthday gift for a friend.

You will need:

Fabric

Scissors

Green lentils

Needle and thread

CARD AND CRÊPE PAPER

Party Hats

aking party hats is a great way of getting the party spirit going. These hats are quite easy to make from card and crêpe paper, and can be decorated with glitter and junk jewelry.

Try your hand at making a complete set of party hats for a special family meal or celebration. Make Queen and King crowns for the grown-ups and fancy coronets or colourful jester's hats for all the children.

You will need:

Thin card

Scissors

Needle and thread

Crêpe paper

Glue

Glitter

Hair band for the tiara

1 Cut a length of card that will go around your head with a small overlap.

2 Next cut a wide piece of crêpe paper the length of the card. This will need to be quite wide; have a look at the illustration to get an idea of the size. Sew a line of running stitch along one of the long sides of the crêpe paper.

3 Glue the crêpe paper onto the card.

Paint pasta shapes gold or silver and decorate with glitter and use to decorate your crown.

4 Next, glue the paper-covered card into a hat shape. Pull the ends of the thread to gather the crêpe paper and tie a knot. Use crêpe paper to cover a small disc shape of card and glue that over the centre of the hat. Decorate the hat with coloured paper or card and glitter.

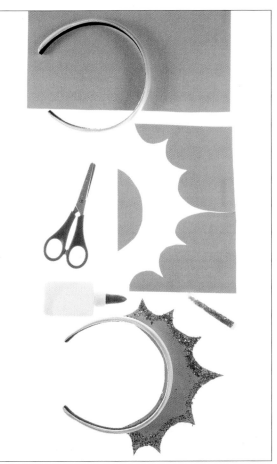

5 This sparkling tiara is made with a hair band and gold card. Lay the hair band onto the card and draw out the shape. Cut out the tiara shape and decorate it with glitter. Attach the tiara to the hair band and leave to dry.

SHOEBOX
Model Theatre

Make a model theatre and stage your own pantomime this Christmas. You will need a shoebox and coloured paper to make the theatre. Once you have decided on a storyline you can get a script together and decorate sheets of paper to use as scenery.

Make small model trees and furnishings from card and paper. Cut out actors from thin card and use sticky tape to attach them to sticks. You can have as many actors on the stage as you can handle. So you may need a friend or two to help when staging your big production.

1 You will need a shoebox to make your theatre. Stand it on its side and cut out an opening on each end. Your actors will enter the stage from these openings.

2 Use coloured paper to decorate the front of the theatre. Make curtains and frills. Use a black felt tip pen to mark out the gathers. Accentuate the edges with glitter.

3 Glue the curtains into place using sticky tape for difficult corners.

4 Cut a piece of paper to size and decorate it with crayons to make a scene that suits your play. Attach it to the back of the box; this will be your scenery backdrop.

5 Cut out coloured paper shapes that match your scenery. Use sticky tape to attach them to the inside edges of the curtains; these are called the wing flats.

6 Draw your actors onto thin card cut out from the lid of the shoebox. Colour them in using felt tip pens and cut them out. Use sticky tape to attach them to the sticks. Remember they will have to enter the stage through the side entrances, so check for height.

Cloth Doll

A soft cloth doll is nice to cuddle up to and looks pretty lying on a pillow as decoration. These dolls are made from cotton fabric and are cut out in a 'gingerbread man' shape. Their hair is made from wool and they are dressed in simply shaped clothes tied with ribbon. A cloth doll can be made large, as a bed decoration or tiny, to live in a doll's house or be a 'pocket' doll. Practise painting faces on a piece of paper to get the shapes right before you paint your doll's face on.

You will need:

Fabric in a flesh colour for the doll

Felt tip pen

Scissors

Needle and thread

Polyester stuffing

Paint

Paint-brush

Wool

Ribbon

Patterned fabric for the doll's dress

1 Draw a doll shape onto a double layer of fabric. Remember you will need a neck shape that you can sew around and cut out. Look carefully at the picture to get an idea of the shape you need to draw.

2 Sew around the drawn line, remembering to leave a gap to turn the fabric out. Fill it with stuffing, then cut the doll shape out.

3 Use the cut-out doll as a pattern to cut a simple dress shape and sew the edges.

4 Turn the dress the right way out and sew a hem along the bottom of the fabric.

5 Dress your doll and paint on a face. Make hair by winding the wool around a piece of card then sewing a 'parting' across the middle. Attach the hair with glue.

6 Tie a ribbon belt in a bow around the waist. Now your doll is ready to enjoy.

Creepy Crawly Pots

Caterpillars, ladybirds, butterflies and flowers make brilliant decorations on small clay pots. These pots are made from air hardening clay in the shape of insects and flowers and painted in summer colours. They are great fun to make. Have a look around the garden for creatures to inspire you before you begin.

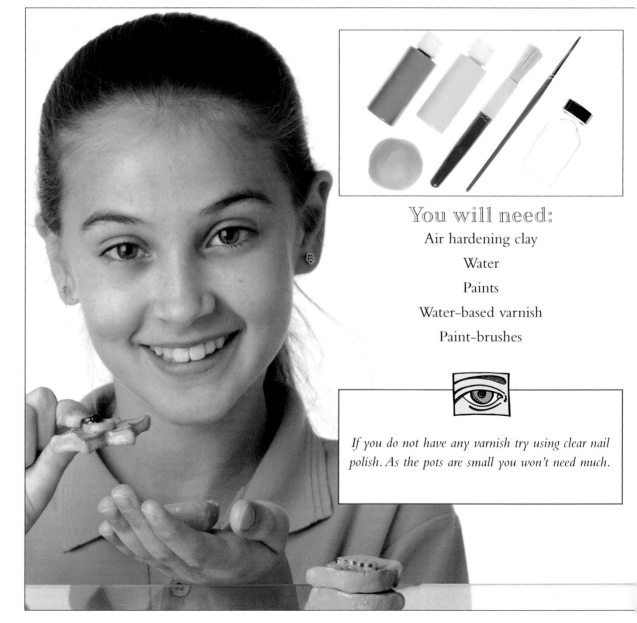

You will need:

Air hardening clay

Water

Paints

Water-based varnish

Paint-brushes

If you do not have any varnish try using clear nail polish. As the pots are small you won't need much.

1 First make the bowl of the pot, using your thumbs to shape it. Smooth the clay with your finger tips. When you are happy with the shape, make a lid to fit the bowl. Gently stretch the lid into petal shapes and make a little ladybird from two small clay balls. Use a little water to moisten the base of the ladybird before you attach it to the lid. Leave the pot in a warm airy spot to dry. When it is completely dry, paint it, allowing the paint to dry between colours. When the paint is dry, varnish your pot to give it a professional finish.

3 The caterpillar on this pot is made from small balls of clay, all joined up with water. When it is dry, decorate the caterpillar in bright colours.

2 This ladybird pot is very easy to make. Make the base first, using your thumbs to shape it and smooth the clay with your fingertips. Make a lid to fit the base and leave the pot in a warm airy spot to dry. When it is completely dry, paint the inside and outside black. When the black is dry, paint the ladybird red, then paint on the black dots. You may need to touch up the black when it is dry.

Découpage Boxes

Découpage is the art of decorating boxes with paper cut-outs. These boxes have been decorated with pictures cut from wrapping paper. Old magazines are a good source for pictures.

Use a box with a tight lid to decorate for a gardening friend to store seeds in, or decorate to hold special handmade decorations for the Christmas tree.

You will need:

Boxes to decorate

Glue

Newspaper

Paint

Paint-brushes

Scissors

Pictures cut from wrapping paper

Water-based varnish

1 Make sure your chosen box is clean inside. Glue on a layer of newspaper squares to cover the box. Leave it in a warm airy spot to dry.

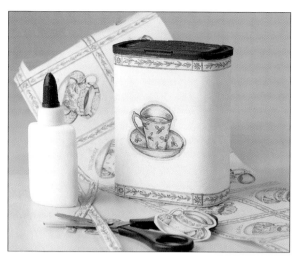

3 When the paint is completely dry, the box is ready to decorate. Cut carefully around the pictures, glue on the border and then the feature picture.

2 When the papier mâché layer is dry, paint on a base coat of colour. You may need two coats to make a good surface to decorate.

4 When the glue is set, the box is ready to varnish. It will need two coats to give it a professional finish.

Decorate small wooden boxes to use for jewelry. Clean up the wood with sandpaper first, then glue on your pictures. Apply two coats of varnish when the glue is dry.

MATCHBOX
Chest of Drawers

The decorations on these tiny chests of drawers give you a good idea of the contents. The chests of drawers are useful for storing stamps or buttons and are made from empty matchboxes, covered with sticky-backed paper. You may want to make a set of drawers for the toolbox to store small nails and screws. The button drawers would be good for saving odd buttons from the sewing box and stamp collectors would find the stamp drawers very useful. You could even make a tiny chest of drawers and decorate it to put in the doll's house bedroom.

You will need:

Empty matchboxes

Glue

Scissors

Sticky-backed paper

Felt

Selection of buttons and stamps

Thin wire (fuse wire would do well)

Saucer of water

Paper fasteners

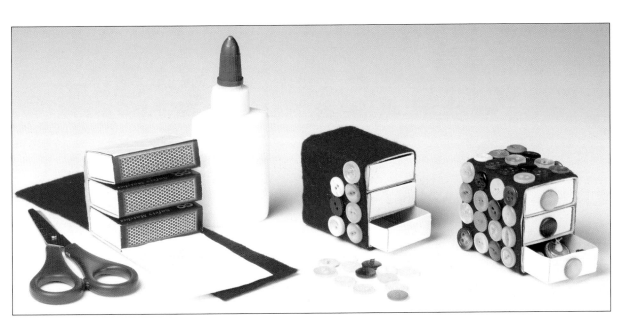

1   To make the button storage drawers, begin by gluing the three matchboxes, one on top of another. When the glue has dried, cover the set of drawers with sticky-backed paper. Spread the box with glue, then stick on the felt covering. Dab on a little glue and stick on the buttons, one at a time. To make handles for the drawers, attach buttons with a little wire.

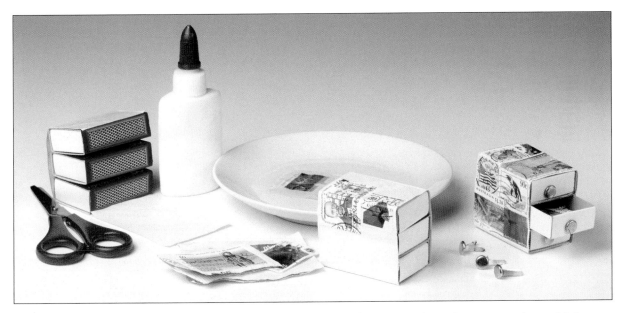

2   To make the stamp drawer you will need a selection of brightly decorated stamps. Place the stamps in a saucer of water for a few minutes to loosen the glue and remove them from the envelope paper. Glue three matchboxes one on top of another then cover the box with sticky-backed paper. Glue on the stamps, taking care to arrange them so you can see the interesting pictures on them. Make drawer handles from paper fasteners.

You could use stickers to decorate a chest of drawers or decorate the sticky-backed paper with felt tip pens.

Money Boxes

These stylishly decorated money boxes would look good in the living room. They are made from recycled containers which have good, well-fitting lids. Encourage the whole family to make savings by decorating money boxes for them all. Flowers painted pink, bright orange and yellow, or a money box that suits a particular hobby or style – you can create them easily from old boxes.

You will need:

Sturdy containers with well-fitting lids

Scissors

Newspaper

Glue

Paint

Paint-brushes

1 You will need an adult to help you cut out the money slit. Use a large coin to help measure the space.

3 When the papier mâché is dry, paint on the base colour, then paint on tiny trees and shrubs.

2 Glue squares of newspaper onto the box to make a good painting surface.

4 These money boxes are made from cardboard boxes. Cut out a slit before covering completely with papier mâché. Once full they will need to be cut open to get at the money!

Pencil Tubs

Use paint and glitter to decorate a useful storage tub for pens and pencils. Choose a cylinder-shaped container to recycle into a pencil tub and cover it with a layer of papier mâché to make it stronger and provide a good surface to decorate.

You will need:

Cardboard containers

Newspaper

Glue

Paint

Glitter

Paint-brushes

Scissors

1 Start by covering the container with a layer of newspaper squares, glued on. Cover the container and leave it in a warm, airy place to dry.

2 When the papier mâché is completely dry, paint on a base coat and allow it to dry. You may need two coats of paint.

3 Paint on the fish and seaweed, using one colour at a time. Don't forget to paint on some air bubbles above the fish.

4 When the paint is dry, spread glue on areas you want to glitter and sprinkle on the glitter. Do this one colour at a time and leave it to dry between colours.

Before you begin, give the cardboard container a quick wash. Stand it upside down to drain and then dry it with a clean tea towel.

Sewing Box

Keep needles and pins, thread and scissors safely to hand in this pretty, fabric-covered sewing box. The box is made from two layers of thick card, each covered with polyester wadding and fabric, and then glued together. When you have mastered the technique you could make a small travel sewing box to match your home sewing box. A fabric-covered box could also be used to hold handkerchiefs, hairbands and scrunchies.

1 Decide on the size of your box. Cut the base from thick card. Use the base to measure out the sides of the box and cut the lid the same size as the base. This will be the outer box. Cut out two complete sets of card. Now cut half a centimetre off around the edge of one set of card pieces. This will be the inner box.

2 Glue a piece of wadding to the four sides of the outer box and cover each one with patterned fabric. Cover the outer lid and base pieces with patterned fabric. Glue a piece of wadding to each piece of the inner box, including the lid and base, then cover these with plain fabric. (Choose co-ordinating fabrics for a stylish effect.)

3 Glue the matching outer and inner pieces together. Glue the whole box together and hold it in place with the elastic band.

You will need:

Thick card

Scissors

Wadding

Half a metre of patterned fabric

Fabric glue

Half a metre of plain fabric

Elastic band

4 To decorate the lid, cover a small square piece of card with plain fabric. Glue this on to the lid. Now cut a strip of fabric, cover it with glue and fold it in half lengthways, roll it up to form a grip, and glue it on to the lid.

Tissue Box Covers

Brighten up a box of tissues with a cover decorated with spring flowers made from coloured paper and card. A daffodil-covered tissue box would make a cheery get-well gift for a friend or relative. Once you have mastered the technique you could decorate a card with a bunch of daffodils to go with the tissue box. A small posy of coloured flowers would look good on a square tissue box.

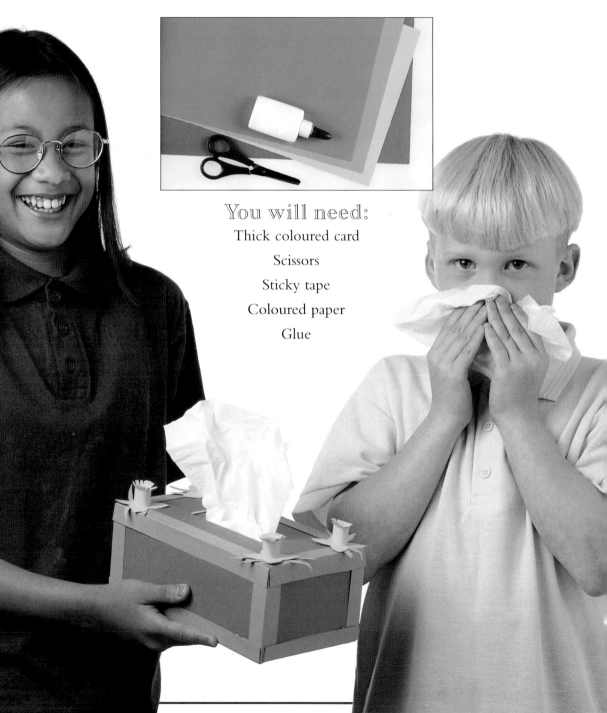

You will need:
Thick coloured card

Scissors

Sticky tape

Coloured paper

Glue

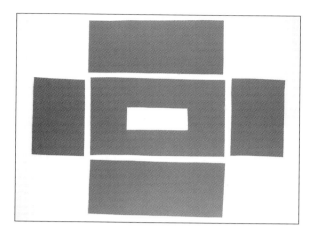

1 Use the tissue box as a pattern and cut out the four sides and top of the cover. Ask an adult to cut a wide slit for the tissues to pull through.

2 Use sticky tape to hold the box together. Cover the sticky tape with decorative edging, cut from coloured paper and stuck on with glue.

3 Cut out the petal shape from yellow paper. Cut out some green leaves. Cut a fringed strip to make the centre of the flower.

4 Shape the fringed strip into the centre of the flower by winding it around your finger. Then glue it in place. Check that the pieces form a well-shaped flower.

5 Glue the flowers and leaves to your finished tissue box cover. Well done!

Cut out and make a few flowers and use the best ones to decorate your tissue box cover. Practise makes perfect!

Toy Boxes

Keep your toys and games tidy in one of these stylishly stencilled toy boxes. Use colours and designs that match your bedroom and make stencils easily from sheets of paper. A nicely stencilled toy box would make a good gift for a younger brother or sister, and older family members might like a well-decorated box to use as a storage container.

You will need rather a lot of glue and paint to cover a grocery box. Check with an adult before you begin to make sure you have enough.

1 Cover the grocery box, inside and out, with two layers of newspaper, glued on. Do this in stages, allowing the box to dry in a warm, airy place between layers.

3 Draw your stencil design onto the centre of a sheet of paper and cut it out carefully. You may want to make a few stencils and try them out on scrap paper.

2 When the papier mâché layer is dry, paint the box. Sometimes a second coat of paint is needed to cover the newspaper. Let the paint dry between coats.

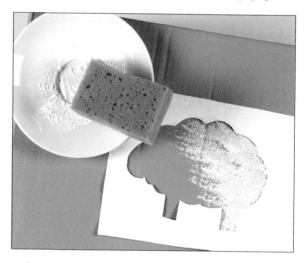

4 Hold the stencil on the box. Dip the sponge into a little paint and pat it on the saucer. Practise on scrap paper before decorating your toy box.

You will need:

Grocery box

Glue

Newspaper

Paint

Paint-brushes

Paper

Scissors

Sponge

Saucer

FOLDED PAPER
Origami

aper folding is a useful skill to learn. Follow the instructions and once you have mastered them, if you have a sheet of paper, you will never be without a box. Use stiff card to make a large box and small sheets of paper to make a smaller one. Origami boxes can be used to store party favours, sweets, wedding confetti and odds and ends. A sturdy, card-folded box could be used as a simple tray to hold biscuits. Have a go, all you need is a sheet of paper and a little practice.

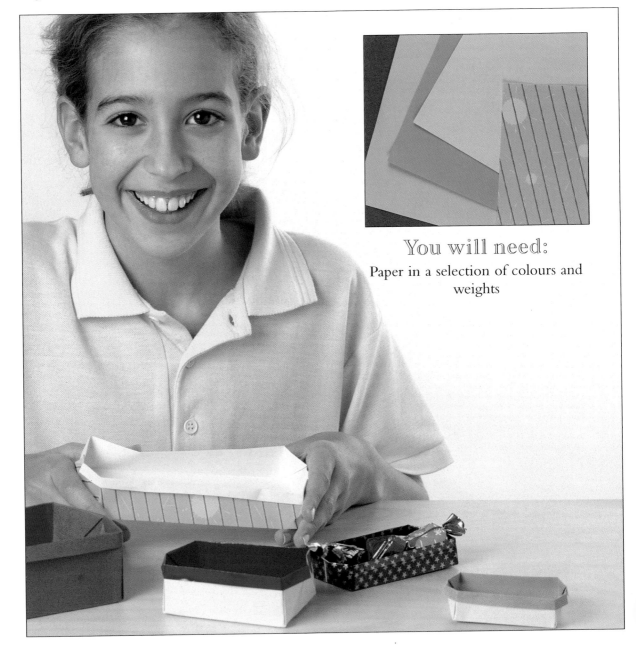

You will need:
Paper in a selection of colours and weights

1 Fold the paper in half lengthways.

2 Fold each half into the middle.

3 Make a small fold back outwards on both sides.

4 Fold in the corners and tuck them under the small fold.

5 Place your fingers in the corners and lift the box into shape.

When paper folding, be sure to press the folds firmly so they are sharp.

CORRUGATED CARD

Woodland Cottage

This little log cottage is just waiting for someone to visit and enjoy the jam tarts and apples set out on the table. The cottage is made from a grocery box and corrugated card. The flowers on the front of the cottage are made from scrunched-up scraps of tissue paper, glued directly on to the walls. When you have made the model, you might try your hand at making some furnishings to put inside the woodland cottage.

You will need:

Corrugated and thick card

Sticky tape

Scissors

Glue

Newspaper

Paint and paint-brushes

Coloured tissue paper

Some plastic pot plants

Oven bake clay

Small rolling pin

1 Decide on the size of your cottage and cut out the base from thick card. Next cut out a front for the cottage. Ask an adult to help if you have difficulty. Cut out the windows and door. Use a wide strip of corrugated card to shape the rest of the cottage.

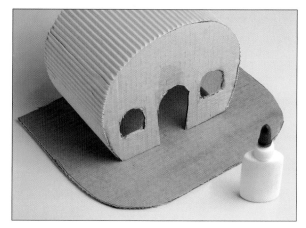

2 Tape the cottage into shape. You may need a little help, one pair of hands to hold things and another pair to attach the sticky tape.

3 Cover the entire model with two layers of newspaper squares, glued on. Leave it in a warm airy place until it is dry.

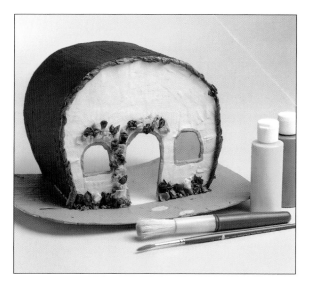

4 Paint the house, allowing each colour to dry before you start on the next one. Use crumpled-up pieces of tissue paper to decorate the house, choosing different colours for the various flowers, and green for leaves. A few plastic plants will give your woodland cottage a realistic feel.

5 The furnishings are made from oven bake clay. Roll it out on a clean surface and shape the log-style bench and table. Make some tiny jam tarts to put on the table.

If you don't have any oven bake clay, use plasticine or modelling clay to make the furnishings and food.

Trinket Boxes

Boxes are great fun to make. These are painted and decorated with glass beads, paints and glitter. Make a box to store your earrings, rings and other small treasures. The square and rectangular boxes are made from recycled grocery box card and the heart-shaped and oval boxes are made from corrugated card. You can sometimes find this as packing or it can be bought in bright colours from a craft shop. The decoration on your box could give a clue as to what is inside it!

You will need:

Thick card

Scissors

Sticky tape

Newspaper

Glue

Paint

Paint-brushes

Corrugated card

Tissue paper

Glitter or glass beads

1 Use cardboard from a grocery box. Decide on the size of your box, then measure out a base and sides. The lid is made from two squares of card, one smaller than the other.

2 Use sticky tape to hold the box together and make sure the lid fits. It will need to be the same size as the base, and the smaller piece of card will need to fit into the box.

3 Cover the box with a layer of papier mâché made from newspaper squares, glued on. Check the lid fits and then leave the box and lid in a warm airy spot to dry before you begin to decorate it with paint.

4 When the papier mâché is quite dry, paint a base coat of colour. You may need to give the box a second coat of paint. Use the point of the brush to paint flowers and leaves on the box and lid, and paint a bright red border.

5 This oval box is made from corrugated card which is easy to bend. Cut an oval shape for the base. The lid will need to be larger than the base, so it fits over the side. This box is covered with coloured tissue paper. Decorate the edge of a heart-shaped box with glitter or glass beads.

PAPER DRAGON
Chinese New Year

The Chinese New Year is a time when families enjoy reunions and gifts, as with so many of the winter festivals. The story goes that once there was a bad dragon who terrorised the people. The people were very frightened but after a while they discovered that the dragon didn't like loud noises, so they all got together and made lots of loud noises. They banged saucepan lids together, shouted and let off firecrackers to frighten him away. Nowadays there is a grand dragon procession with fireworks and many people holding up a giant paper dragon. After the event families join together to eat specially prepared meals to welcome in the New Year. They give gifts of money wrapped in red envelopes to each other. The Chinese New Year begins with a new moon, and it is also the time when the farmers gave thanks for the harvest. Have fun making your own small Chinese dragon and if there are a few of you, why not make lots of dragons so you can have your own Chinese New Year procession.

You will need:

Thin card

Felt tip pens

Glitter

Glue

Scissors

Tissue paper

Paper

Sticky tape

Two sticks

1 Draw a dragon's head onto a piece of thin card. Use felt tip pens to colour and decorate it with glitter.

4 Make the body by taking two strips of paper and folding them one over the other repeatedly to make a concertina.

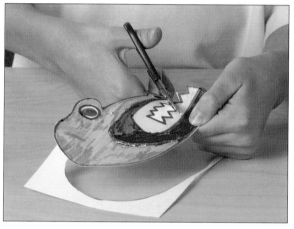

2 Cut out the dragon's head carefully.

5 Attach paper ribbons to the dragon's tail. Glue the head to the other end of the body.

3 Cut strips of tissue paper to use as ribbons. Use the glue to stick these paper ribbons to the dragon's head.

6 Use sticky tape to attach the sticks to the dragon's body. One is for the head and the other for the tail.

St. Valentine's Day

You will need a heart shaped biscuit cutter to make both the picture frames and the gingerbread hearts! Both will make great Valentine gifts to give to friends and sweethearts. The gingerbread biscuits are simple to make and can be decorated with icing or left plain. Either way they are delicious to eat. The heart shaped picture frame has space for two pictures. It is made by rolling out the clay and using two biscuit cutters to cut the frame, one smaller than the other. A coat of varnish (or clear nail polish) will give your picture frame a professional finish.

You will need:

Air hardening clay

Heart biscuit cutter

Red paint

Paint-brush

Thread or ribbon

Glue

Recipe for gingerbread biscuits

350g plain flour

1 teaspoon baking powder

2 teaspoons ground ginger

1 teaspoon cinnamon

100gm margarine

175gm soft brown sugar

3 tablespoons syrup

1 egg

Icing

1 Place the flour, baking powder, ginger, cinnamon and sugar in a large bowl. Add the margarine, mix it in well with your fingertips until the mixture looks crumbly like breadcrumbs.

2 Add the sugar and syrup, mix together. Use a spoon to stir in the egg and mix.

3 Turn the mixture out onto the work surface and knead the mixture until it is smooth and well mixed. Sprinkle some flour onto the work surface and use the rolling pin to roll the mixture out to a thickness of about half a centimetre. With a heart shaped biscuit cutter cut out the shapes. Place the shapes on a baking tray and bake at 170°C, 325°F, gas mark 3 for just 10 minutes. Get an adult to help you use the oven.

4 When the gingerbread biscuits are cooked take them out of the oven and leave to stand until cold. They will harden up as they cool. When they are cool, decorate the biscuits with icing.

5 To make these picture frames you will need two biscuit cutters, one smaller than the other, and some air hardening clay. Roll out the clay and cut out two large heart shapes. One of the heart shapes will be the picture frame back. Take the smaller heart shaped biscuit cutter and cut a small heart shape out of the second heart shape. Leave the made frame pieces to dry in a warm airy place. When they have dried completely, paint them with red paint and glue them together. Place a picture of your Valentine in the frame. Use glue to secure it to the frame.

The heart-shaped frames look good enough to eat, but remember they are made from air hardening clay and are not edible!

Easter

In the Northern hemisphere Easter occurs in the springtime, so we have Easter bunnies, eggs and spring flowers, such as the daffodils on this delightful Easter card. It is fun to make and grandparents will enjoy receiving greeting cards at this time of year. The chocolate nests are made from breakfast cereal and melted chocolate. The tiny eggs are chocolate covered raisins, or, instead, you could use small foil covered chocolate Easter eggs. Another fun Easter activity is to make an Easter tree. This tree is made from a branch and decorated with paper Easter eggs.

You will need:

Shredded breakfast cereal

Bowl

Melted chocolate

Spoon

Foil

Bun tin

Chocolate covered raisins

1 Crumble the cereal by hand into a bowl.
Check that there are no large chunks.

2 Carefully add the melted chocolate to the
bowl of crumbled cereal and, using the
spoon, mix well together.

3 Line a bun tin with foil and place a
spoonful of the mixture into each space.
Use the back of the spoon to press it
down into a nest shape. Leave the shapes
to harden in a cool, dry place.

4 When the nests are hard, put them on a
plate and add a few chocolate covered
raisins to each one. Serve up at tea time
on Easter Sunday.

5 A branch decorated with paper Easter
eggs will brighten up the home. Cut the
Easter eggs from paper and decorate them
using pencil crayons. Make a hole at one
end of each egg and thread with string to
hang them on the Easter tree.

6 Use coloured paper to make this Easter
card. The daffodils have bright yellow
paper petals and a paler yellow centre.
Cut the leaves from green paper. Use glue
to attach the flowers to the card.

HOME MADE SOUP AND BREAD
Harvest Supper

Harvest is a special time of year. It comes at the end of summer when the farmers have harvested all the summer grown crops, ready to store for winter use. After harvest, wheat is ground into flour for bread and the kitchens of vegetable gardeners are full to overflowing. We have prepared a pot of soup using a mixture of seasonal vegetables and made some bread rolls and a loaf to enjoy with the soup. Ask an adult to supervise the cooking and make a special family harvest supper.

You will need:

A packet bread mix

Bowl

A little extra flour

Baking tray

Egg

Pastry brush

Rack

Soup ingredients

Knife

Large saucepan and water

Fork

Small soup bowl

Soup recipe:

1 onion

2 sticks of celery

2 medium potatoes

2 large carrots

1 leek

A vegetable stock cube

1 teaspoon of mixed herbs

A squeeze of tomato purée

A little oil

Salt and pepper to taste

Always check with an adult before using the cooker.

1 Follow the directions on the bread mix packet. You will need to pour the packet mix into a bowl and add the required quantity of water. Mix well with a spoon until the mixture forms a dough.

4 When the bread is ready it will smell delicious and be a lovely golden brown colour. Ask an adult to help take the bread out of the oven. Place the cooked bread on a rack to cool.

2 Sprinkle the work surface with a little flour. Empty the dough onto the work surface and use your hands to knead it. After a few minutes you will see and feel that the dough becomes smooth. When it is all smooth to touch and eye, you can begin to shape it.

5 Chop up the vegetables before you begin to make the soup. Place all the ingredients into a large saucepan. Pour enough water into the saucepan to cover the ingredients. Bring to the boil and then turn down the heat so the soup cooks gently. Allow to cook for half an hour.

3 Divide it in two sections and shape it into bread rolls and a plaited loaf. Place them on a baking tray. Brush with beaten egg and leave in a warm spot to rise. When the dough has doubled in size, bake according to the instructions on the packet.

6 Ask an adult to help. Prick some of the vegetables with a fork to make sure they are cooked. Season with salt and pepper if necessary. Serve in a small soup bowl and enjoy your soup with your freshly baked harvest bread and rolls.

SAND AND PETAL PICTURE
Diwali

Followers of the Hindu religion celebrate many festivals. Diwali or the Festival of Light is my favourite Hindu festival. Diwali is celebrated around October/November time and is a New Year celebration. In Hindu homes the house is cleaned and decorated with coloured glitter, sand and flowers. Lots of small clay lamps are kept burning on windowsills and on doorsteps. These lights are to welcome Lakshmi, the goddess of wealth. Everyone hopes she will visit them over this period and bring good fortune for the New Year. Many Hindu homes in India have sand pictures drawn up outside their front doors to welcome visitors. Make a sand and flower picture to place in your hall during Diwali.

You will need:
Air hardening clay
Paint-brush and paint
Paper and pencil
Glue stick
Coloured sand
Flower petals
Glitter

Before you use a candle make sure you have an adult present.

1 To make your Diwali lamp you will need a ball of air hardening clay. Use your fingers to shape it into a bowl shape and press a fancy edge into the clay. When the lamp has dried, paint it in bright colours and decorate with gold or silver paint. Place a nightlight candle in the lamp and check with an adult before you light it.

2 You will need a large piece of paper. Use a pencil to sketch a flower picture onto the paper. Use a glue stick to mark the centre of the flower.

3 Pour coloured sand onto the glue mark.

4 Next use the glue stick to mark out the shape of the petals.

5 Pour coloured sand onto the glue lines.

6 When you have completed the sand picture place flower petals as a border.

7 Use glitter to add the finishing touch to your Diwali picture.

LANTERNS, GAMES AND CREATURES
Hallowe'en

Hallowe'en is a spooky time of year. Make a hollowed-out pumpkin lantern. Carve a face on one side of the pumpkin and stand it outside your home with a lit candle inside. The golden candle light will shine through the dark! For ghoulish fun try making this very squidgy Hallowe'en game. Your friends will enjoy plenty of laughs searching the green gunge for spiders and worms. The glow-in-the-dark character worm is made from oven bake glow clay. You could make some to put in trick or treat boxes. Open them in the dark to enjoy the glow!

1 Half fill a large bowl with water. Add enough food colouring to turn the water dark green. Sprinkle 3 or 4 tablespoons of wallpaper glue onto the water. Allow the wallpaper glue to sink to the bottom and then stir gently with the spoon until the mixture is sloppy and thick.

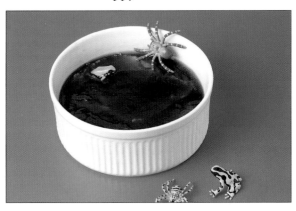

2 Add the spiders and toads and the game is ready to play. Take turns to feel through the gunge and guess which creature you are fishing out.

3 Make the cute little glow-in-the-dark worm with special oven bake glow clay. Make the body first, then form it into the worm shape. Make a number of small ball shapes in dark green and flatten them. Press them onto the worm. Make a hat and place it on the worm's head. Bake the completed model according to the manufacturer's instructions. You could stand the finished worm on a shelf as an ornament or turn him into a fridge magnet or brooch.

You will need:

Bowl

Water

Green food colouring

Wallpaper glue

A selection of plastic toads and spiders

Oven bake glow clay

Pumpkin

Knife

Candle

TREE DECORATIONS
Christmas Time

When the Christmas tree goes up we know Christmas is definitely on the way. Presents will soon be piling up underneath it and excitement is in the air. Spend an afternoon making some of these decorations to hang on your tree. You can use card and paper, glitter and string to make these keepsake decorations. The tiny angels are made from rice and pasta shapes, glued together and painted gold. They are quite easy for even tiny hands to make.

You will need:

Dried pasta quill and bow shapes

Glue

Small wooden balls or beads to use as angel heads

Rice

Gold thread

Gold paint and paint-brush

Paper or gold tissue paper

Poppy seedheads

Thin metallic card

Glitter

If you do not have glitter glue, make your own. Use PVA glue and mix in an equal amount of fine glitter.

1 Use strong glue to stick the pasta shapes together. Begin with a quill shape, this will be the angel body. A bow shape will make the angel wings, glue this onto the quill. Glue a wooden ball on as a head and a few grains of rice as hair, and a loop of thread to hang the angel onto the tree. When the glue has dried firmly, decorate the angel with gold paint.

3 Save some poppy seedheads in the summer. Dry them and when Christmas comes round turn them into beautiful baubles. Cut away the stems and glue on a loop of gold thread to hang the decoration onto the tree. Paint the seedhead gold and when dry you will have a lovely tree decoration.

2 This shower of gold stars looks very pretty hanging on the Christmas tree. Cut star shapes from gold tissue paper or plain paper painted gold. Glue the stars onto long pieces of gold thread and then drape them over the Christmas tree. These stars would also look good draped across the mantlepiece, shimmering in the light.

4 These colourful baubles are cut out of thin metallic card. Use a paper punch to make a hole for the loop of thread and decorate the baubles with strips of metallic card and glitter.

GIFT CALENDAR
Advent

The twenty four days before Christmas are marked by an Advent calendar. This calendar is made from a sheet of painted chipboard. Hammer twenty four tacks into the decorated board and on each tack hang a small gift. You can fill small boxes with a mixture of home made gifts and bought trinkets. Chocolate or other sweets would be suitable Advent gifts to wrap and hang up on the calendar. You might want to make an Advent calendar for a younger brother or sister to hang in their own room as sharing the treats may be difficult!

1 Paint one side of the chipboard a rich dark blue. It may need more than one coat.

4 Hammer twenty four tacks into the board. Space them out evenly.

2 Use a sponge dipped in silver paint to decorate the edges of the board.

3 Cut a star shape from the centre of a piece of paper and use it as a stencil. Use the sponge and silver paint to stencil stars attractively across the blue painted board.

5 Use brightly coloured tissue paper and gold thread to wrap up all twenty four small gifts you have collected. Hang the gifts up on the board and your Advent calendar is ready to use.

You will need:

Piece of chipboard

Paint and paint-brush

Sponge and saucer

Paper

Scissors

Hammer and twenty four tacks

Small gifts

Tissue paper

Gold thread

OVEN BAKE CLAY

Thanksgiving

Thanksgiving is a special festival that has been celebrated every year in the United States of America since about 1620. The Pilgrim settlers who sailed across the Atlantic ocean in wooden sailing boats, arrived in America and established their colony in 1620. Their first winter was hard and they had very little to eat and many of them died from sickness. In the spring the friendly Native American people brought them food and taught them which herbs and plants were good as medicine and food. The Native Americans helped the settlers plant crops of corn and other vegetables which grew well in America. When the crops were harvested in the autumn and the people knew they had enough food to last through the next winter they were very pleased. The first Thanksgiving took place and the people gave thanks to God for the harvest.

This miniature thanksgiving meal is made from oven hardening clay. You will need green, buff and orange clay.

1 The miniature turkey and roast potatoes are made from buff coloured oven hardening clay. Shape the turkey's body first then add the drumsticks. Make quite a few roast potato shapes to go around the turkey. Roll out tiny green peas (you will need an awful lot of them!) and carrots from orange clay. Place the pieces on an baking tray and bake according to the manufacturer's instructions.

2 To make the pumpkin pie you will need a layer of buff clay (for the pastry base) and a layer of orange (for the pumpkin filling). You might want to make impressions along the outside edge of the pie to give the look of a pastry case. Place a ball of white clay as cream in the centre of the pie. Bake the pie in the oven according to the manufacturer's instructions.

3 Once your Thanksgiving meal is ready assemble all the pieces on some plates cut from a piece of thin card.

Christmas Day

Home made Christmas crackers are one of the many things you can make in advance in preparation for Christmas. Fill them with paper hats, jokes (good ones!) and small gifts which you could make, such as necklaces or small brooches or badges. Paper hats are easy to make from tissue paper. You will need to fold them up small so they fit in the crackers. The snaps are available from craft shops. You might want to make a special cracker for a grandparent or friend you won't be seeing over the Christmas season. Send it to them through the post so that they can pull it while they are enjoying their Christmas dinner.

You will need:

Tissue paper, for hat and cracker

Scissors

Thin card

Sticky tape

Small gift to put inside the cracker

Snaps

Glue

Glitter

You could use the central cardboard cylinder from a roll of toilet paper to shape your crackers.

1 Before you make the cracker you will need to make a tissue paper hat. Use your own head to make a standard size hat. If you are making the hat to fit an adult-head, make it a little larger. Cut a zig-zag shape along one side, and glue the two short edges together.

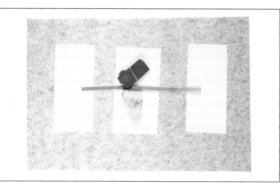

2 To make the cracker you will need a sheet of tissue paper measuring 40cm x 20cm and three pieces of thin card measuring 14cm x 8cm. Add a snap, a paper hat tightly folded, and a small gift.

3 Roll the pieces of thin card into cylinder shapes. Hold them in place with sticky tape. Run the snap through the cylinders and place the hat and gift in the central cylinder.

4 Roll the tissue paper around the cylinders and use thread to tie in between them. Pull up the thread firmly to create the cracker shape. Remove the two end cylinders and trim any excess paper away.

5 The cracker is ready to decorate. Use glitter and glue on a seasonal picture.

CAKES

Special Days

These novelty cakes look great on a party table and would make a surprise birthday gift to take to a party. The icing is simply rolled out with a rolling pin then placed over the cake. The decorative pieces are cut using biscuit cutters which come in so many shapes and sizes you are sure to find one to suit the style of cake you want to make. Use a bought-in sponge cake to ice or make your own following the easy recipe below. Ask an adult for help when you use the cooker.

Sponge cake:

75gm self raising flour

75gm castor sugar

75gm margarine

2 eggs

1 tablespoon water

1 Sieve some icing sugar onto your work surface so that the icing doesn't stick to it and roll out the icing to about half a centimetre thickness.

2 Roll the icing over the rolling pin and, lifting it gently, transfer it to the cake. Drape it over the cake and carefully remove the rolling pin.

3 Gently press the icing over the cake. Cut away any excess icing with a knife. Use a clean cloth to wipe away any icing sugar.

4 Roll out some red icing and use a biscuit cutter to cut out the star shapes. Moisten the back of the stars with a little water and press them gently onto the iced cake.

5 Use different shaped biscuit cutters to create different styles of cake. Green frogs, red stars or blue fish could be cut out and decorated further with silver balls or edible felt tip colours. Have fun creating your own designs to suit different occasions.

You will need

Sponge cakes to ice

Icing sugar

Rolling pin

Easy-roll icing

Knife

Clean cloth

Small sieve

Biscuit cutters

A little water and a pastry brush

Index